GARDENING
IN THE
INLAND NORTHWEST

GARDENING
IN THE
INLAND NORTHWEST

A Guide to Growing Vegetables, Berries, Grapes and Fruit Trees

BY
TONIE JEAN FITZGERALD

ILLUSTRATED BY
ELLEN FITZGERALD HOKANSON

YE GALLEON PRESS
FAIRFIELD, WASHINGTON

Additional copies of this book may be ordered from:
Arboreal Press
954 East 14th
Spokane, Washington 99202
(509) 534-1304

Library of Congress Cataloging in Publication Data

Fitzgerald, Tonie Jean.
  Gardening in the inland Northwest.

  Includes index.
  1.   Vegetable   gardening — Northwest,   Pacific.   2.   Fruit-
culture — Northwest, Pacific. I. Title. II. Title: Inland Northwest.
SB321.F58 1984   634'.09795   84-27046
ISBN 0-87770-343-4

Dedicated to my husband, Greg Plunkett,
whose patience with the things that really matter always tops mine.

I would like to thank friends Marilyn, Melissa, Doug, and Paul for their encouragement and help in editing.

I would also like to commend the Spokane County Master Gardener Volunteers with whom I had the pleasure and privilege of working and whose dedication to community service has inspired me in my gardening and writing efforts.

TABLE OF CONTENTS

INTRODUCTION

I wrote this book for people in the Inland Northwest who want to grow vegetables, fruits, berries and grapes but who don't wish to become certified horticulturists in the process. It is a simple, straightforward book about which varieties grow here, when to plant them, how to plant them, and what to do about the bugs and diseases that pester them.

There are dozens of gardening books packed with general gardening information which can be used by anyone, regardless of where he or she lives. These are good reference sources and they supplement local garden know-how. They also fill out a bookcase well. Every serious gardener has some.

Then there are the Pacific Northwest gardening books which are great if you live "over there" near the Pacific Ocean with balmy winters and cool, drizzly summers. But we don't.

Gardening in the Inland Northwest is about gardening in this large region lying between the Cascade and Rocky Mountain Ranges and stretching from Canada down through Oregon.

I have garnered information from regional universities, the U.S. Weather Bureau, managers of nurseries, veteran gardeners, gardening friends and, of course, personal experience.

Gardening in the Inland Northwest contains basic information necessary for gardening here, including lists of plant varieties, planting dates, local growing conditions, and common pests and problems.

PART ONE

THE BASICS

THE INLAND NORTHWEST CLIMATE

The Inland Northwest stretches from Canada down through Oregon, bordered on the west by the Cascade Mountains and on the east by the Rocky Mountains. A large air mass lies trapped between the two mountain ranges and is cooled by the region's northern latitude. These conditions make for cold, long-lasting winters and hot, relatively short summers. This is the land of nine months of winter and three months of bad skiing.

In planning their gardens, Inland Northwest residents must consider the length of the growing season, the daily weather patterns during the growing season, and local micro-climates.

The length of the growing season is the time between the last frost in the spring and the first one in the fall. Every year, the U.S. Weather Bureau (listed under U.S. Department of Commerce in your phone book) records the first and last frost dates for areas throughout the country. The Inland Northwest, like all large regions, includes several areas with varying growing seasons.

Some areas within the Inland Northwest have fewer than eighty frost-free days during the year. Gardeners in these areas, undoubtedly skiers, use short-season varieties of fruits and vegetables and rely on plant protectors during much of the gardening season to ward off damaging frosts and cold weather.

Most Inland Northwest gardeners work around a 100- to 150-day growing season, but a fortunate few, residing in the banana-belt regions of south central Washington, north central Oregon and a sliver of land southwest of Boise, Idaho, can easily grow hot weather yummies such as watermelons, cantaloupes, and wine grapes. Their frost-free season is upwards of 180 days.

The daily weather patterns during the growing season include such things as high and low temperatures and the amount of rainfall and sunshine. Because the Inland Northwest region is not tempered by moist ocean breezes, it is subject to extreme temperatures, sudden temperature changes and great fluctuation during a 24-hour period.

Any summer night may get cold enough to cause frost in the morning while the same afternoon may get hot enough to wilt plants. Rainfall during the summer is infrequent, resulting in many clear, sunny days (good for gardening) and water stress (bad for gardening). Inland Northwest gardeners are always on their toes.

Generalizations can be made about the growing season and weather patterns, but view them only as generalizations. Conditions vary because of a crucial factor to home gardeners called the "micro-climate."

A micro-climate is a small area within a larger area which has different growing conditions from the larger area. Micro-climates are affected by elevation, exposure, proximity to a building or a body of water, slope of the land, and other local conditions. For example, the space just beneath a south-facing wall may collect enough heat to grow grapes while an area several feet away wouldn't get hot enough to mature a short-season tomato. The grapes are growing in a warm micro-climate near the wall.

Other examples of warm micro-climates include south-facing slopes of land, spaces next to buildings or fences which are protected from the wind and exposed to the sun, and areas which are higher than surrounding land so that cold air, being heavier than warm air, flows downward to the surrounding low-lying areas.

Cold micro-climates include north-facing slopes of land, areas shaded by north-facing structures, and low-lying areas that collect cold air and frosts.

Find out more about local growing conditions from gardening neighbors and employees of nurseries and agricultural agencies. By tempering government data with neighborhood gospel, you'll soon learn what it takes to garden in your part of the Inland Northwest.

Table I lists several Inland Northwest cities and towns and their average growing season figures. Use these as a guide but don't underestimate the importance of micro-climates which can lengthen or shorten the growing season by a few weeks or more.

14

TABLE I

Average Growing Seasons in Inland Northwest Cities and Towns.

TOWN	AVERAGE # DAYS	TOWN	AVERAGE # DAYS
WASHINGTON		**IDAHO**	
Cheney	150	Boise	150
Colville	110	Bonners Ferry	100
Deer Park	110	Coeur d'Alene	100
Ellensburg	120	Gibbonsville	80
Goldendale	170	Grangeville	120
Grand Coulee	130	Idaho Falls	120
Moses Lake	140	Kellogg	110
Newport	90	Lewiston	150
Othello	180	McCall	90
Prosser	180	Moscow	130
Pullman	120-150	Mt. Home	110
Ritzville	150	Nampa	150
Spokane	120-150	Orofino	150
Tonasket	150	Pocatello	120
Tri-Cities	180-200	Priest River	90
Walla Walla	200	St. Maries	100
Wenatchee	150-180	Salmon	95
Yakima	165-180	Sandpoint	100
		Twin Falls	130
		Wallace	110
OREGON		**MONTANA**	
Baker	100	Anaconda	90
Bend	90	Bozeman	120
Burns	100	Butte	90
Canyon City	90	Helena	90
Condon	120	Kalispell	120
The Dalles	180	Libby	70
Enterprise	100	Missoula	90
Heppner	160	Superior	90
John Day	90		
La Grande	120		
Madras	100		
Milton-Freewater	190		
Ontario	180		
Pendleton	160		
Prineville	90		

15

SOIL: Know Your Underground

In the art of gardening, soil is where it's all happening. Soil is a reservoir for air, water, and nutrients which are all needed for plant growth. Soil is also a recycling center for organic matter which is essential for soil structure and fertility. Fungi, bacteria, worms, and insects reside in the soil and do the recycling work.

It is the relative amounts of all the soil components—air, water, minerals, organic matter, and living organisms—which determine the soil type and whether it's a good or bad prospect for gardening. One of our jobs as gardeners is to maintain a good balance between drainage, aeration, and soil fertility.

A major component of soil is mineral or rock material. The size of rock particles determines the soil texture which, in turn, affects soil drainage, and aeration. Clay particles are the smallest rock particles. They are flat and closely packed together. Sand particles are large, blocky particles remaining loose and gritty. Silt particles are between clay and sand in form and size. Silt feels almost powdery to the touch.

No soil is all one type of mineral. Clay soils contain 60% clay particles and 40% sand/silt mixture. Sandy soil is about 85% sand particles and 15% silt/clay mixture. The best garden soil is a type called loam with 40% sand, 40% silt, and 20% clay. And then there are sandy loams, silt loams, etc.

Clay and very sandy soils are bad prospects for gardening and both types exist in the Inland Northwest. In clay, water clings tightly around each tiny particle, creating a "heavy" soil. Gardeners with heavy clay soil have a problem. In the spring they wonder if the ground will ever dry out enough to walk across without hip boots. Later in the summer when it does dry out, clay-soil gardeners find they have something akin to cement. Drainage is poor, air is virtually absent and nutrients, though present, are locked in place.

The opposite condition exists in sandy or rocky soil. Many Inland Northwest gardeners, especially Spokane Valley residents will attest to this. Gardeners in the Valley do not refer to their soil as sandy. They simply call it sand. Or rocks. Water quickly evaporates or drains away, carrying nutrients with it and leaving gardeners with high water bills and dry ground. Only air is in good supply, which is why sandy soils are referred to as "light."

A redeeming quality of rocky soil is that rocks retain heat, allowing the ground to warm up quickly in the spring. That's why "rock gardeners" enjoy a somewhat longer growing season than the rest of us. It's small compensation, though, for having to spend years building up bits of soil between the stones.

The answer to all this woe is organic matter. Organic matter is a major component in good, fertile soil, but where it is in short supply, it should be added. In clay, it breaks up the packed particles, creates air spaces and improves drainage. In sand, it binds together loose particles and helps retain water and nutrients.

Organic matter is the raw material for humus which makes soil dark, moist and fertile. Humus is anything that was once living — roots, leaves, worms, mushrooms — and is now in some stage of decay. It's rotten stuff, really, and it works wonders in the ground.

Grass clippings, leaves, straw, manure and sawdust are all sources of organic matter. The smaller the materials, the faster they help the soil. That's why it's best to improve the soil with composted materials (See "Making Compost") or ready-made products such as peat moss, Perma-Mulch, Jacklin Organic Mulch, Eko-Compost or Soil Aid.

Pine needles, though abundant in the Inland Northwest, aren't a great source of organic matter. Even when shredded they take years to decompose and provide little nutritive value.

Enriching soil by adding organic matter is a continuous process. It is never finished because organic matter eventually breaks down into nutrients, carbon dioxide and water, all of which are utilized by plants.

Organic matter, though expendable, is the best tool for improving the soil and increasing gardening success. Replenish the garden annually with organic matter.

17

FERTILIZERS

If organic matter adds nutrients and improves the soil, why does one need to fertilize a garden?

Because. Plants need more than what organic matter has to offer. They need large amounts of nutrients and they need it fast when they're ready to grow in the spring. Commercial fertilizers meet these needs. Decaying organic matter does release nutrients, but it is a slow process in which small amounts of nutrients are released over a long period of time. It is also a temperature dependent process which means it doesn't happen until the soil warms up to about 70 or 80 degrees.

So, we buy fertilizers to feed the plants.

Plants need three major elements and several trace elements. Trace elements, or micro-nutrients, are used in minute amounts and practically every good garden soil contains enough to supply plants with what they need.

On the other hand, plants use large amounts of nitrogen, phosphorous, and potassium, and particularly nitrogen. These are the major elements which need replacing on a yearly basis.

No matter how much you understand soil fertility, one look at all the available fertilizer products will have you floundering. There are dozens of names, number combinations, and types of fertilizers, including organic and inorganic types, all claiming to be exactly what plants need.

Basically, all commercial fertilizer products are sold as a combination of nitrogen (chemical symbol "N"), phosphorous (chemical symbol "P"), and potassium (chemical symbol "K"). Usually, there are three numbers on the fertilizer bags which refer to the percentages of N, P, and K in that order. So, a bag of 10-10-10 contains 10% N, 10% P, and 10% K and a bag of 21-0-0 contains 21% N, and no P or K. Sometimes a fourth number appears. It represents the percentage of sulfur in the mix. The number sequence is called the fertilizer analysis.

How Much Fertilizer to Use

Most bags of fertilizer come with the instructions printed right on the bag for how much to apply to a lawn or garden. To avoid the arithmetic blues, look around for those bags.

If you're a do-it-yourselfer or a generic brand buyer, you'll need to know these things about computing fertilizer rates:

1) Fertilizer rates are usually figured according to the amount of nitrogen needed.

2) Pounds of nitrogen does not equal pounds of fertilizer. Each fertilizer product has only a certain percentage of nitrogen. For instance, 10-20-20 is 10% N so ten pounds of the fertilizer contains 10% or one pound nitrogen. Likewise, 21-0-0 is 20% N (roughly), so five pounds contains 20% or one pound nitrogen.

3) Rates are usually determined for a 100- or 1000-square foot area. Measure your garden to determine its square footage and figure accordingly.

Vegetable and flower gardens require one pound N per 1000 square feet. If your garden is 500 square feet, you'll need a half pound N; if it is 1500 square feet, you'll need one and a half pounds, and so on.

It is tedious, but if instructions aren't on the bag, it's better to spend some time figuring than to ruin your plants with too little or too much fertilizer. You know, better safe than sorry.

Table II lists several common garden fertilizers found in garden stores. The column on the right shows how many pounds of fertilizer to apply to a 1000-square foot area to supply one pound of nitrogen. The formula is:

$$100 \div \% \text{ N} = \text{pounds fertilizer needed to supply one pound N.}$$

TABLE II

Fertilizer Product Name	Analysis (% N, P, K)	# Pounds Needed To Supply 1 lb. N *
Alaska Fish Fertilizer	5-1-1	applied in solution
All Organic Plant Food	5-3-1	20
Ammonium nitrate	33-0-0	3
Ammonium sulfate	21-0-0	5
Bone Meal (raw)	3-15-0	33
Chicken Manure	3-2-2	33
Cottonseed Meal	7-2-1	14
Grow Vegetables	18-24-6	5½
Lilly Miller Tomato & Vegetable Food	4-8-6	25
Milorganite (activated sewage sludge)	6-2-0	16
Miracle-Gro for Tomatoes	18-18-21	applied in solution
Morcrop	10-20-20	10
Ortho Tomato & Vegetable Food	6-18-6	16
Peters Professional Fertilizer	20-20-20	applied in solution
P.F.C.	18-10-10	5½
Planting & Growing Food	8-12-8	12½
Power to Grow for Lawns & Gardens	23-7-14	4½
Rapid Grow	23-19-17	applied in solution
Steer Manure	.7-.7-.7	145
Superphosphate	0-18-0	doesn't supply N
Super Rich Lawn Fertilizer	12-3-16	8½
Ultra Green Lawn Fertilizer	24-2-5	4
Unipel	16-16-16	6
Urea	44-0-0	2½

* One pound of a granular fertilizer is about equal to 2 cups.

As for using organic (natural) fertilizers vs. inorganic (synthetic) ones, there are pros and cons with each type. Organic types, such as sterilized manure, bone meal, cottonseed meal, and fish emulsions are excellent plant foods containing trace elements as well as N, P, and K. Organic fertilizers remain in the soil longer than synthetic types, but nutrients from organic substances are not available to plants until soil micro-organisms partially eat and break them down into usable forms. This occurs after the soil warms to about 70 degrees.

Inorganic fertilizers, on the other hand, are cheaper, easier to handle, and contain more nutrients per unit weight than organic types. For example, five pounds of 21-0-0 contains the same amount of N as fifty pounds of cattle manure or thirty-three pounds of raw bone meal. Synthetic fertilizers are not dependent on microbial breakdown and are readily available to plants.

A combination of the two types is most beneficial to the soil; however, plants will eventually get what they need from either organic or synthetic fertilizers. For best results, use fast acting synthetic fertilizers in the early spring when temperatures are cool and use organic products later in the summer after the soil has warmed.

Many eastern Washington and northern Idaho soils contain high levels of P and K. Gardeners whose soil tests verify this soil condition have successfully used 21-0-0 (ammonium sulfate) in lawns and vegetable gardens. Being one of the cheapest of fertilizers, this is a particularly attractive buy. Without a soil test, it may be safer to use a *complete* fertilizer with N, P, and K such as 21-3-3, 21-7-14, 10-10-10, etc.

SOIL pH:
Everything you always wanted to know, and more . . .

The pH value. You hear about it in things like shampoo and hemistry experiments. So, what does it have to do with gardening?

Soil pH is a measure of soil acidity or alkalinity and it affects the availability of nutrients to plants. In very acid or alkaline soil, the work of micro-organisms is inhibited and important elements such as iron, phosphorous and potassium are tied up.

Neutral soils have a pH of 7.0. Acid soils have pH values between 0 and 7.0 and alkaline soils have pH values between 7.0 and 14.0. A soil test is needed to determine the pH value.

Most Inland Northwest soils range from slightly acid to slightly alkaline. This is okay for growing most vegetables and correction is not necessary.

Some areas have soil pH levels above 7.8 which should be corrected with applications of sulfur or acid-forming fertilizers to create optimum growing conditions for plants. Sulfur lowers the pH and makes the soil less alkaline.

A few areas in the Inland Northwest have acidic soils which should be corrected with lime. Lime raises the pH and makes soil less acidic.

Do not use lime or sulfur unless a soil test shows the need for them.

Vegetables grow best within a pH range of 5.5 to 7.0. Vegetables can and do make it in soils with pH levels above or below that range, but they may be stunded, yellow or otherwise unhealthy.

Guidelines for working with pH levels are these:

pH 5.5 or lower: Too acid. Add 50 pounds ground limestone or 35 pounds hydrated lime per 1000 square feet. Hardwood ashes (not pine or fir) at the rate of 10 to 15 pounds per 1000 feet may slightly reduce soil acidity but should not be used where potassium levels are high.

pH 5.5 to 7.0: Optimum range. No correction needed.

pH 7.0 to 7.8: Slightly alkaline. Okay for plants but use ammonium fertilizers such as ammonium sulfate, ammonium nitrate, urea, or cottonseed meal or peat moss.

pH above 7.8: Too alkaline. Add 50 pounds of elemental sulfur per 1000 square feet.

If either lime or sulfur is necessary, apply it in the fall to the top of the soil. The winter rains will dissolve the material and move it through the soil.

Do not use lime for any other reason than to raise soil pH. Lime, by itself, does not control diseases, kill moss, stop mushrooms or anything else.

Pine needles are often heralded as acid-forming materials. The fact is that pine needles, when mixed into the ground, break down very slowly and don't alter the pH to any measurable extent. They are okay as a mulch between rows but should not be worked into the soil.

SOIL TESTING:
Knowing for Sure

The surest way of getting what your garden needs and not wasting money on superfluous additives is to have a soil test done. Do-it-yourself kits are available at most garden centers for about fifteen dollars. They give a ballpark figure for soil pH and fertility. Several soil samples can be analyzed with one kit.

A more accurate analysis can be obtained by sending a soil sample to a soil testing laboratory. Do it in the fall or early spring so you'll have results in time to do something about them.

Check the yellow pages of the phone book for "Laboratories" and call to see if they'll do home garden analyses. Most are commercial labs and a home garden analysis may be cost prohibitive.

A better option is to check with your county extension office about sending samples to the state university soil testing laboratory. The cost for a one-time test runs about fifteen dollars. You'll get back an official looking form with readings for soil pH, nutrient levels and other things. They're designed for agricultural use but the information can be used for gardens too.

The following is a list of county extension offices and phone numbers in the Inland Northwest.

Washington State Cooperative Extension Service

Adams County
210 W. Broadway
Ritzville, WA 99169
(659-0090)

Benton County
1121 Dudley Ave.
Prosser, WA 99350
(843-3701)

Columbia County
Federal Building
202 South Second St.
Dayton, WA 99328
(382-4741)

Asotin County
Courthouse Annex
P O Box 9
Asotin, WA 99402
(243-4118)

Chelan County
400 Washington St.
Wenatchee, WA 98801
Pasco, WA 99301
(545-3511)

Cowlitz County
Courthouse Annex
Kelso, WA 99626
(577-3014)

Douglas County
Courthouse
Box 550
Waterville, WA 98858
(745-8531)

Kittitas County
Courthouse
5th and Main
Ellensburg, WA 98926
(962-6811)

Spokane County
N. 222 Havana
Spokane, WA 99202
(456-3651)

Ferry County
Courthouse
P O Box 345
Republic, WA 99166
(775-3161)

Klickitat County
210 Courthouse Annex
228 W. Main
Goldendale, WA 98620
(773-5817)

Stevens County
P O Building, Box 32
Colville, WA 99114
(684-2588)

Franklin County
Courthouse
Pasco, WA 99301
(545-3511)

Lincoln County
Box 399
Davenport, WA 99122
(725-4171)

Walla Walla County
314 Main St.
Walla Walla, WA 99362
(525-7930)

Garfield, County
Courthouse
Pomeroy, WA 99347
(843-3701)

Okanogan County
Courthouse
Okanogan, WA 98840
(422-3670)

Whitman County
Public Service Building
310 N. Main
Colfax, WA 99111
(397-3401)

Grant County
Courthouse
Ephrata, WA 98823
(754-2011)

Pend Oreille County
Federal Building
Box 5000
Newport, WA 99156
(447-3325)

Yakima County
233 Courthouse
Yakima, WA 98901
(575-4218)

Oregon State Cooperative Extension

Baker County
2610 Grove St.
Baker, OR 97814
(523-6414)

Harney County
450 N. Buena Vista
Burns, OR 97720
(575-2506)

Morrow County
P O Box 397
Heppner, OR 97836
(676-9642)

Crook County
Courthouse
Prineville, OR 97754
(447-6228)

Jefferson County
530 D Street
Madras, OR 97741
(475-3808)

Sherman County
P O Box 385
Moro, OR 97039
(565-3230)

Gilliam County
P O Box 707
Condon, OR 97823
(384-2271)

Lake County
Courthouse
Lakeview, OR 97630
(947-2279)

Umatilla County
13 S.W. Nye
Pendleton, OR 97801
(276-7111)

Grant County
Courthouse
Canyon City, OR 97820
(575-1911)

Malheur County
P O Box 397
Ontario, OR 97954
(676-9642)

Union County
R R 1 Box 705
LaGrande, OR 97850
(963-8686)

25

Wallowa County
P O Box 280
Enterprise, OR 97828
(426-3143)

Wasco County
P O Box 821
The Dalles, OR 97058
(296-5494)

Wheeler County
P O Box 407
Fossil, OR 97830
(763-4115)

Idaho Cooperative Extension Service

Ada County
5880 Glenwood Ave.
Boise, ID 83704
(377-2107)

Canyon County
Box 1058
1115 Albany St.
Caldwell, ID 83605
(459-1654)

Latah County
Courthouse Room 209
Moscow, ID 83843
(882-8580)

Adams County
Box 43, Courthouse
Council, ID 83612
(253-4279)

Clearwater County
Rt. 2 Box 7 E
Orofino, ID 83544
(476-4434)

Nez Perce County
1225 Idaho St.
Lewiston, ID 83501
(799-3096)

Benewah County
Box 189 Courthouse
St. Maries, ID 83861
(245-2422)

Gem County
2199 S. Johns
Emmett, ID 83617
(365-6363)

Payette County
Box 10, Federal Bldg.
Payette, ID 83661
(642-9397)

Bonner County
Box 1526, Fairgrounds
Sandpoint, ID 83864
(263-8511)

Idaho County
Courthouse, Room 3
Grangeville, ID 83530
(983-2667)

Valley County
Box 337, Scheline Bldg.
Donnelly, ID 83615
(325-8566)

Boundary County
Box 267, Courthouse
Bonners Ferry, ID 83805
(267-3235)

Kootenai County
106-2 Dalton Ave.
Coeur d'Alene, ID 83814
(667-6426)

Washington County
485 Third
Weiser, ID 83672
(549-0415)

Montana State Cooperative Extension Service

Flathead County
723 5th Ave East
Kalispell, MT 59901
(755-5300)

Lincoln County
418 Mineral Ave.
Libby, MT 59923
(293-7781)

Missoula County
301 W. Alder
Missoula, MT 59801
(721-5700)

Lake County
P O Box 0
Ronan, MT 59864
(676-4271)

Mineral County
P O Box 730
Superior, MT 59872
(822-4561)

Sanders County
P O Box 189
Thompson Falls, MT
59873
(827-3532)

26

PART TWO

VEGETABLE GARDENING

E. Hokanson

CHOOSING A GARDEN SITE
And What To Do If You Don't Have One

Before you even THINK about starting a garden, make sure you have the right place to put it. Vegetables need at least six hours of sunlight and a good place to hang their roots, meaning ground with good drainage. The drainage situation can be improved with organic matter and raised beds, but shady spots will always spell trouble.

There are a few alternatives if you don't have an ideal garden spot:

1) Grow vegetables in separate, small areas that do get full sunlight. Put tomatoes along a south side wall or fence, put lettuce or cabbage along a walkway, put beans in a sunny corner of the yard. This plan will keep you on the move but vegetables don't mind being in separate places.

2) Rent space in a community garden program. Plots range in size from small to large and are rented on a yearly basis. Spokane's community garden, called City Farms, has provided space for hundreds of people since 1975. Other cities and towns also have community gardens. Find out about them from park departments, neighborhood centers, food co-ops, or other community service agencies.

3) Plant vegetables in containers on the patio, porch steps or balcony. Tubs, buckets, planter boxes and clay pots are all suitable containers. Poke drainage holes in the bottom and fill them with a light, porous soil mixture; regular dirt from your yard will get too compacted during the season. Plant the seeds or transplants, set them in a sunny spot, and stand back. With regular watering and fertilizing, container vegetables grow fast.

Trellises, available at most garden centers, support vining plants such as beans, peas, tomatoes and squash. In containers, these plants grow vertically better than they do sprawling on the ground.

Examples of vegetable varieties particularly suited to life in a bucket include:

Tiny Tim Tomato, Basket King Tomato, Small Fry

29

Tomato, Gypsy Hybrid Pepper, Tom Thumb Butterhead Thumb Butterhead Lettuce, Spacesaver Cucumber, Bush Crop Cucumber, New York Improved Eggplant, Slim Jim Eggplant, Alpine Strawberry and Sweetheart Strawberry. Small vegatable and herb plants such as radishes, chives, short carrots, and beets also work well in containers. New varieties come out every year, so there will always be several choices.

Don't let lack of space keep you from enjoying fresh, own-grown vegatables. Where there's a will there's a way!

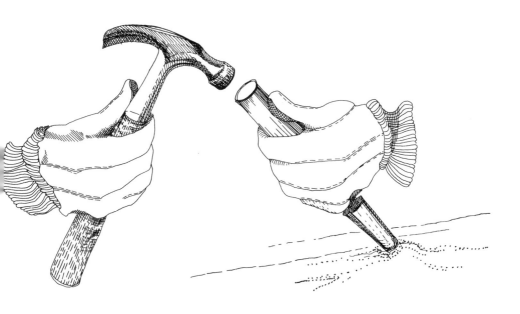

BREAKING GROUND

Digging up the garden is traditionally a job saved for the first nice, spring day. Unfortunately, the thrill of the occasion causes a lot of people to work overzealously and end up with debilitating backaches. (The author knows this because the author has done it.) Be sensible about heaving that shovel around. Don't do more than your back can handle at one time. It helps to take breaks during the job, lie flat on the ground and lift both knees to your chest to stretch the lower back.

All right, enough physical therapy . . .

The purpose of preparing the soil is threefold: to get rid of sod or weeds; to loosen the ground for drainage, aeration, and root growth; and to add organic matter and fertilizer.

31

Removing Sod And Weeds

If your chosen garden site is currently a lawn, don't despair. Removing sod, especially a lot of it, is an abominable task, but you only have to do it once and compared to the amount of time you'll garden in that space, removing the sod is a short investment in time and labor.

Sod cutters (machines, not people) can be rented for ten or twelve dollars an hour. The hardest part of using a sod cutter is getting the thing on and off the pick-up truck. It's about the size of a lawn mower, but much heavier.

Sod cutters raze 12- to 18-inch strips of sod which can be rolled up or cut into squares and stacked. If it's good turf material, use it somewhere else in the yard or advertise in the paper to sell it. You could recover the cost of renting the machine. If neither option interests you, heave the sod into the compost pile. With time, it makes excellent compost.

If the sod cutter is you and not a machine, use a square-end spade or shovel to cut out sections of sod. Fifteen-inch squares are easy to work with. Lift the sod by grasping one corner of the squares and pulling backwards. Shake off loose soil from the grass roots and toss the pieces on a wheelbarrow for transport to the next destination.

"Bare ground" is usually growing at least one crop of weeds. Getting rid of those weeds is your task at hand before planting a garden. In most cases, hand-pulling and hoeing the weeds is the best eradicating method. The little ones can be scraped and pulled out with a hoe, but larger, deep-rooted ones will take some hacking. Try to extract whole roots because remaining pieces may sprout new weeds. Ideally, you should weed a garden plot a couple of times in early spring before planting seeds.

A few weed killer products or herbicides are available to make the job easier for large or hopelessly weedy areas. Round-up is registered for use on already-growing weeds, but not all vegetables can be planted in Round-up treated areas. Be sure to use the product according to label directions.

Dacthal is another garden weed product that can be used in some instances in the vegetable garden. It works as a pre-emergent herbicide, meaning it kills weed seeds as they germinate. Dacthal is used around vegetable transplants and prior to planting of large seeded vegetables, such as beans and peas, which germinate above the ground. Weeder is another brand name for Dacthal. Again, read the entire label of weed killers before using them on a vegetable garden (or anywhere else).

Loosening Up The Soil

With sod and weeds gone from your garden plot, it's now time to loosen the soil and add organic matter. Organic matter can be applied to the soil in the fall but new gardens benefit from the soil amendment in the spring.

Rototillers make digging a garden a breeze, but it's not hard to do it with a shovel and hoe either.

Use a shovel to dig down into the ground and loosen it. The deeper you go, the better, but twelve inches should be the minimum for adequate drainage and aeration. This is the time to be adding old manure (old enough so it doesn't look or smell like manure), compost, or other organic matter to the soil. Refer to the soil chapter for sources of organic matter.

Next, take a hoe and go back over the dug-up area and start chopping at the clods of earth, breaking them into smaller and smaller pieces. At the same time, incorporate the organic matter uniformly throughout the soil. (Remember, use your leg and arm muscles, not just your back.) The hoe brings to light rocks and other buried objects. Toss these to the edge of the garden as you work. The end result should be a loose, crumbly soil, free of weeds, large rocks, sticks and man-made objects.

Adding Fertilizer

Generally speaking, vegetable gardens need a pound of nitrogen per 1000 square feet. The fertilizer chapter explains the different kinds of fertilizers and the list on page 20 shows how many pounds of each kind supply one pound of nitrogen.

Fertilizer should be applied in the spring, prior to seeding. Broadcasting the fertilizer is the easiest way of applying it. Measure the desired amount into a coffee can. Then shake the granules, as uniformly as possible, over the garden area. Next, use a rake to mix the granules throughout the top few inches of soil.

In row gardens, fertilize the whole garden area. Later on, if necessary, fertilizer can be sidebanded along each row of vegetables. (see page 64.)

For raised bed gardens, wait until the beds are formed before applying fertilizer. It isn't necessary to have fertilizer in the walkways between beds.

Ideally, you should run a sprinkler over the garden and let water dissolve some of the fertilizer a day or two before seeding. You can, however, plant seeds or transplants immediately after fertilizing if the fertilizer is well mixed into the soil.

PLANNING A GARDEN STYLE AND PLANTING IT

Gardening is not without style and currently there are two from which you can choose. There is the traditional row garden in which vegetables are planted in long, straight rows between footpaths. These are easy to plant and are the best choice for large gardens.

Then there is the "raised bed" style. Gardening in raised beds is actually a very ancient concept, but it has become increasingly popular in recent years. It's also known as intensive gardening—so called because you plant vegetables close to each other and produce more food per unit area than in row gardens.

Planting in raised beds is desirable when soil compaction or drainage is a problem. Also, the soil in raised beds warms up earlier in the spring, lengthening the gardening season by a week or more.

Some gardening books have elaborate plans for building attractive, permanent beds with railroad ties or bricks. You can reach the same objective, with less work and expense, by mounding loose soil up with a hoe to form beds, keeping eighteen-inch walkways between them. A little bit of "re-structuring" is all that's required to maintain the beds every year.

Whichever style you choose, be sure to measure the garden space, draw it on paper and plan to scale the layout of the rows or beds. Planting a garden without a plan is like doing anything without a plan—it just doesn't work as well.

Start with knowing the square footage of your garden. Then, look on seed packets of the vegetables you want to plant and determine how much space each one needs *at maturity*. Usually, seed packets have information on how far apart to plant seeds as well as how much space to leave between plants after thinning them. The distance between plants after thinning is how much space they'll need to mature. This information may not seem important for smaller vegetables such as carrots, but it is crucial in planning how many cabbages, squash, tomatoes or other large vegetables to plant.

Planting Row Gardens

The easiest way to mark a row is to tie a long string between two stakes. Place the stakes at each end of the planned row, pulling the string taut. With the edge of a hoe, make a furrow for the seeds using the string as a guide.

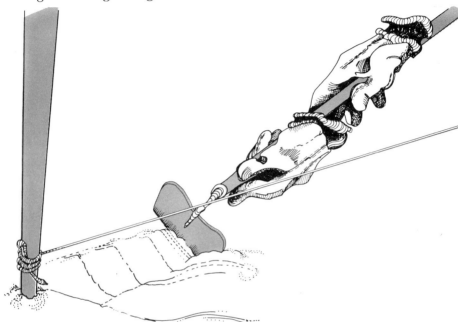

If there's a noticeable slope to the land, make the rows against it so that water doesn't make rivers and gullies in the walkways during rainstorms or watering. Otherwise, an east-west or a north-south or even a diagonal direction to the rows doesn't make much difference as long as tall corn or tomato plants don't shade out the shorties like lettuce or bush beans. Tall plants on the south side of a garden will cast shadows over shorter plants to the north.

Plant seeds according to depth and spacing recommended on the seed packet. Tamp the seeds down lightly with a hoe and then cover them with loose soil. Put a labeled stake (with water-insoluble ink!) at one end of the row so that you remember what you planted there before pulling up the marking string to move on to the next row.

Some soils, particularly if they've been rototilled, are almost fluffy after preparation. Place a long board between the rows to stand and walk on to prevent deep footprints and holes.

Finally, lightly sprinkle the planted garden just enough to moisten the surface of the soil. Do this daily, or as needed, until seeds germinate. Then switch to longer, less frequent waterings.

Planting Raised-Bed Gardens

After loosening the ground a foot or more in depth, form raised beds by mounding soil up with a hoe so that it is about eight inches above the level of the walkways. Make walkways about eighteen inches wide and never step into the beds once they are formed.

The width of the beds depends on the length of your arms. From the walkway you should be able to reach comfortably into the middle of the bed for planting, weeding and harvesting. Three feet is a typical width for raised beds, but narrower beds may be a more comfortable reach for you.

When a bed is formed, measure its width and length and determine the amount of fertilizer needed for that area. Scatter the granules uniformly over the bed. With a hoe or rake, mix the fertilizer into the top few inches and then flatten the top of the bed.

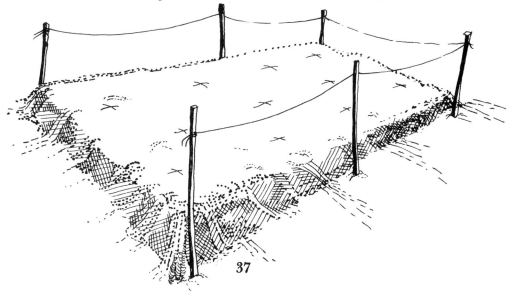

37

Because the soil in raised beds doesn't get compacted from walking between individual rows, plants can be grown closely together and still get the water and nutrients they need. Transplants and large seeds (e.g. peas, beans, spinach and beets) go into these raised beds in a pattern like the dots on a ten-spot domino.

For spacing, use the seed packet information regarding space between plants, but not distance between rows. For example, in row gardens, beans should be planted four to six inches apart in rows twenty-four inches apart. In raised beds, all the beans should be planted four to six inches apart in a solid block. This solid planting conserves water and requires little weeding once the plants start filling out.

It's tedious planting tiny seeds such as lettuce and carrots one at a time. Broadcast tiny seeds over the top of the beds and cover the seeded area with a quarter-inch of loose soil or a soil/sand mixture. Later, thin the seedlings out as they crowd each other.

Finally, lightly sprinkle the planted beds as recommended for row gardens.

Both styles of gardens benefit from the use of plastic film on the ground prior to planting seeds or transplants. The plastic raises the soil temperature in the spring, keeps weeds down and conserves soil moisture throughout the season. (see "Mulching" on page 60.)

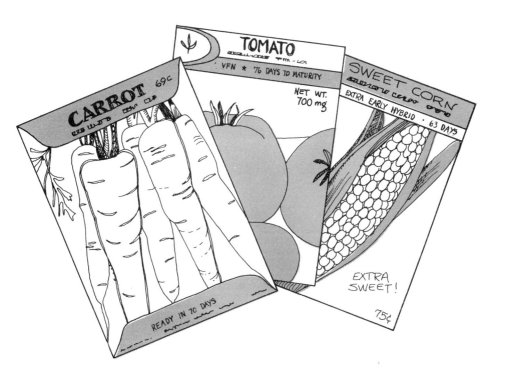

CHOOSING VEGETABLE VARIETIES

Vegetables come in many varieties, making it possible to choose, among other things, the size, shape, and date of ripening of your garden bounty. Varietal differences make shopping for vegetables interesting and can lead to some intriguing experiments for the curious gardener.

Most varietal characteristics are a matter of personal choice, but some can add to your gardening success. For instance:

1) Days to maturity: All seed packets have this number printed somewhere on the envelope. This is how long it takes from planting the seed until harvest. For vegetables that must be transplanted, the number is closer to the days from transplanting outside till harvest. (For example, tomatoes with 75-day maturity dates will mature 75 days after transplanting, not 75 days from seeding inside.) Consider this information carefully when selecting

frost-tender vegetables such as tomatoes, corn, peppers, and melons. Vegetables suited for short-season gardening are often labeled as "early" varieties.

2) VFN: Tomato seeds or transplants are often labeled VFN, meaning they are resistant to Verticillium Wilt and Fusarium Wilt, two hard-to-control fungus diseases, and Nematode worms. Nematodes are rarely a problem in the Inland Northwest, but Verticillium and Fusarium diseases may be, especially where tomatoes, potatoes, strawberries and raspberries have been grown for several years.

3) Mosaic Resistant: Cucumbers, melons, squash, beans and peppers are susceptible to virus diseases causing yellow and green mosaic patterns on the leaves. Buying mosaic resistant varieties of these vegetables is advisable if you see the problem recurring.

4) Disease Resistant: Many vegetables are labeled as "disease resistant." Common diseases in the Inland Northwest that warrant your concern include powdery mildew, rusts, and potato scab.

5) Heat Resistant or Slow Bolting: Lettuce, spinach, broccoli and cauliflower are subject to bolting, or going to seed once hot weather sets in. Some varieties of these plants are made to be heat resistant so they'll last longer in the garden.

6) Bush-type or Spacesaver: Standard sized cucumbers, squash, pumpkins, and tomatoes have a way of taking up too much space in the garden. Bush-type or Spacesaver varieties of these and other vegetable plants are advisable for small or container gardens.

7) Hybrids: In order to provide the above qualities and more, plant breeders cross-breed some vegetables to foster some characteristics and inhibit others. F_1 means the seed is a first generation of a cross. Hybrid seeds produce true-to-kind vegetables only once. Don't save seeds from them. Seeds from hybrids are a genetic mixture and won't produce the same plant again.

The following list of vegetable varieties was compiled from recommendations of Spokane and Pend Oreille County Master Gardeners, area nursery employees and other veteran gardeners. It is not an exclusive list—there are certainly many other varieties which may do well in your garden. This list is intended only as a guideline.

The numbers following the variety names are the days-to-maturity figures. All varieties are listed in order of ripening; if you live in a short-season area, choose the earlier maturing varieties.

The days-to-maturity are based on average figures and harvest time will vary somewhat from year to year. Also, different seed companies may give different figures for the same vegetable variety. Hence, Burpee Seed Co. lists Buttercrunch lettuce as a 75-day crop and Johnny's Selected Seeds lists Buttercrunch lettuce as a 50-day crop. This is an extreme case. Generally the figures are close enough not to make a significant difference in your garden plans.

ASPARAGUS:
 Mary Washington (matures 2 years after planting.)
BEANS:
 Bush Types: Early Contender (40), Tendergreen (45), Provider (50), Topcrop (50), Royal Burgandy (51), Roma (53), Blue Lake Bush (55), Royal Deep Purple (55), Pencil Pod Wax (55), Kentucky Wonder Bush (58), Bush Romano (60), Dwarf Horticultural (68).
 Pole Types: Romano (60), Blue Lake (60), Kentucky Wonder (65), Horticultural Pole (70).
 Dry Beans: Dwarf Horticultural (65), Black Valentine (70), Broad Windsor (70), Envy Soybeans (75), Fava (85).
BEETS:
 Early Red Ball (48), Ruby Queen (52), Golden Beet (55), Early Wonder (55), Cylindra (60), Red Ball (60), Lutz Greenleaf (60), Detroit Dark Red (63).
BROCCOLI:
 Early Spartan (52), Green Comet (55), Green Goliath (55), Bonanza (55), Italian Sprouting (55), Premium Crop Hybrid (60), Green Sprouting (65), Waltham 29 (70).
BRUSSEL SPROUTS
 Jade Cross Hybrid (85), Long Island Improved (90), Jade Cross (100).
CABBAGE:
 Earliana (60), Early Jersey Wakefield (63), Golden Acre (64), Copenhagen Market (68), Stonehead Hybrid (70), Ruby Ball (red) (70), Red Acre, (red) (85), Late Flat Dutch (105), Danish Ballhead (105). Chinese cabbage varieties mature in about 70 days.
CANTALOUPES:
 Far North (65), Minnesota Midget (65), Alaska (70), Early Sweet (70), Sweet 'n' Early Hybrid (75), Burpee Hybrid (82), Short 'n' Sweet (90),

41

Rocky Ford (95), Hearts O'Gold (95).

CARROTS:
Little Fingers (65), Nantes (65), Ladyfingers (66), Short 'n' Sweet (68), Chantenay (70), Danvers Half Long (75), Imperator (75), Tendersweet (75). (Short varieties are best for heavy soil.)

CAULIFLOWER:
Mini Snow (42), Snow King Hybrid (50), Early White Hybrid (52), Self-Blanching (68), Early Snowball (70), Purple Head (80).

CHARD:
Rhubarb (60), Lucullus (60), Fordhook Giant (60).

CORN:
Seneca (60), Early Hybrid Giant (63), Early Sunglo (63), Early Golden Giant (63), Early Extra Sweet (71), Golden Cross Bantam (73), Honey & Cream (78), Bantam (80), Illini Xtra Sweet (83), Iochief (86), Kandy Korn (89), FM Hybrid.

CUCUMBERS:
Burpee Pickler (53), Burpee Hybrid (55), Bush Whopper (55), Straight-8 (58), Spacemaster (60), Long Marketer (60), Armenian (70).

EGGPLANT:
Early Black Egg (65), Burpee Hybrid (70), Black Magic (70), New Hampshire (70), Japanese Long Purple (75), Midnite Hybrid (75), Black Beauty (80).

ENDIVE:
Green Curled (90), Escarole (90).

GARLIC:
All varieties planted in fall mature in mid-summer.

KALE:
Dwarf Blue Scotch (55), Dwarf Blue Curled (55).

KOHLRABI:
Early White Vienna (50), Early Purple Vienna (55).

LETTUCE:
Leaf Types (more heat tolerant than bibb or head types): Grand Rapid (43), Black Seed Simpson (45), Green Ice (45), Oakleaf (46), Ruby (47), Prizehead (48), Royal Oakleaf (50), Salad Bowl (50).
Bibb Types: Summer Bib (57), Buttercrunch (60), Tom Thumb (65), Dark Green Boston (80).
Head Types: Iceberg (85), Great Lakes (90).
Romaine Types: Winter Density (60), Romaine (60), Paris White Cos (80).

OKRA:
Lee (50), Dwarf Long Green Pod (52), Clemson Spineless (56).

ONIONS:
Sets of all varieties mature in about 75-80 days. *Seeds*: Early Yellow Globe (100), Red Hamburger (100), Yellow Ebenezer (100), Walla Walla Sweet

(110), Sweet Spanish (110), Evergreen Long White Bunching (120).

PEAS:

Edible Pod: Sugar Bon (56), Sugar Ann (58), Oregon Sugar Pod (68), Sugar Snap (70).

Shell Pea: Early Alaska (55), Home Freezer (57), Progress (60), Early Frosty (63), Little Marvel (63), Blue Bantam (64), Dwarf Early Grey (65), Novella (70), Green Arrow (70).

PEPPERS:

Green Bell types: Ace (50), Merrimac (60), Gypsy Hybrid (65), Early Cal Wonder (69), Bell Boy (72), Cal Wonder (75), Tasty Hybrid (75), Yolo Wonder (76).

Other types: Hungarian Hot Wax (58), Early Jalapeno (65), Hungarian Wax (70), Sweet Banana (72), Jalapeno (75), Anaheim (77).

POTATOES:

Tubers mature when plants turn yellow and dry. Red Pontiac, Dakota, Russet Burbank, Norland, Netted Gem, Irish Cobbler, Butte, Norgold Russet, Kennebec.

PUMPKINS:

Cinderella (95), Small Sugar (100), Jack O'Lantern (110).

RADISHES:

French Breakfast (23), Cherry Belle (24), Early Scarlet (24), Sparkler White Tip (25), Champion (28), White Icicle (30), Crimson Giant (30).

RHUBARB:

MacDonald, Victoria, Valentine, Ruby, Strawberry. All varieties mature 2 years after planting.

RUTABAGA:

American Purple Top (90), Laurentian (90).

SALSIFY:

Mammoth (120).

SPINACH:

Melody (42), Avon Hybrid (44), Northland Thickleaf (50), Bloomsdale Longstanding (50), Fordhook (70), New Zealand (70).

SQUASH:

Summer types: Peter Pan (50), Straightneck (50), Scallopini (50), Zucchini (50), Gold Rush (52), Yellow Crookneck (53).

Winter types: Butterbush (75), Early Acorn (75), Early Butternut (75), Acorn (80), Bush Table Queen (80), Butter Boy (80), Jersey Golden Acorn (80), Sweet Mama (85), Sweet Meat (85), Buttercup (90), Spaghetti (100), Hubbard (120).

TOMATOES:

Cherry Tomatoes: Patio Hybrid (50), Small Fry (52), Tiny Tim (55), Gardener's Delight (65), Sugarlump (68), Sweet 100 (70).

Standard: Sub Arctic varieties, (53-61), Patio Pixie (52), Toy Boy (55),

Early Pick (62), Early Girl (62), Big Early (62), Early Cascade (63), Earliana (65), Nova (65), Fantastic (70), Spokane Valley Pride (70), Yellow Pear (70), Golden Jubilee (72), Better Boy (72), Rutgers (74), Roma (75), Floramerica (75), Bonny Best (78), Big Boy (78), Big Girl (78), Beefmaster (78), Longkeeper (78).

TURNIP:

Purple Top White Globe (50), Royal Crown (54), Globe Purple Top (55).

WATERMELON:

New Hampshire Midget (70), Garden Baby (74), Ford Hook Hybrid (74), Sugar Baby (80), Bush Baby Hybrid (80), Sweet Favorite (82).

WHEN TO PLANT WHAT
Cool Season and Warm Season Vegetables

Read the small print on the backs of seed packets and you'll find it says, "PLANT COOL SEASON VEGETABLES AS SOON AS SOIL CAN BE WORKED . . ." Clear as mud, right? Here are some clues for knowing when soil is workable:

— You can walk across it without making *schlurping* sounds.
— You can squeeze a handful of it and it doesn't squirt out between your fingers.
— You can hoe or dig in it without forming big, mucky clumps.

There may be other tests. The point is that you have to wait for the ground to dry out a little before planting even the earliest of early season seeds. They will only rot in cold, wet soil.

Elsewhere in small print on seed packets you'll find, "PLANT WARM SEASON PLANTS AFTER ALL DANGER OF FROST IS PAST." (If you doubt that there is such a time in your area, refer to the chapter on Extending the Season, page 56).

Inland Northwest gardeners can, on the average, expect the last spring frost to occur sometime between May 1st and June 1st. Check with local gardeners, nurseries, and agricultural agencies to pinpoint the frost dates for your specific area.

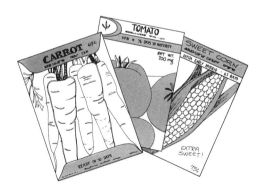

Cool season vegetables are rugged individuals capable of germinating in soil temperatures as low as 40°. They grow and mature during the cool weather of spring and early summer. Cool season vegetables are:

LEAFY TYPES	ROOT TYPES	OTHERS
Lettuce	Beets	Peas
Spinach	Carrots	Broccoli
Chard	Radishes	Cauliflower
Mustard	Parsnips	Brussel sprouts
Endive	Turnips	Onions
Kale	Salsify	Potatoes
Cabbage	Jerusalem	Asparagus
Chinese cabbage	artichokes	Rhubarb
		Chives

Warm season vegetables are fussier. They need soil warmth to germinate—at least 60°—and long, warm days to mature. Warm season plants, bearing the large, fleshy vegetables are:

Beans	Eggplants	Pumpkins
Corn	Melons	Squash
Cucumbers	Okra	Tomatoes
	Peppers	

The following planting dates are guidelines that Spokane gardeners use. Most Inland Northwest places are not too far ahead or behind this schedule, but gardeners in the coolest areas should modify their planting schedule by a week or so because of later last-frost dates in the spring and/or earlier ones in the fall.

MARCH 1st:

    Indoors: start cabbage, cauliflower, broccoli, Brussel sprouts, and pepper seeds.

    Outdoors: plant dried onion bulblets, called *sets*, or small green onion plants, and Jerusalem artichokes.

APRIL 1st to 15th:

    Indoors: start tomato and eggplant seeds.

    Outdoors: plant radishes, peas, lettuce, spinach and other leafy greens; asparagus roots, rhubarb roots, chives.

APRIL 15th to MAY 1st:

    Indoors: start cucumber, melon and squash seeds.

    Outdoors: plant beets, carrots, turnips, and other root crops; potato pieces. Transplant cabbage, cauliflower, broccoli, and Brussel sprouts.

MAY 15th to JUNE 1st:

    Outdoors: plant beans and corn. Be prepared to replant these if frost occurs. Transplant cucumbers, melons, and squash.

JUNE 1st to 15th:

    Outdoors: transplant tomatoes, peppers and eggplant. Plant okra seed.

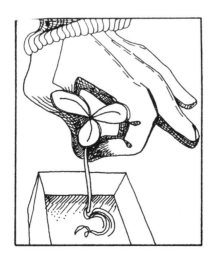

TRANSPLANTING:
Helping the Non-Hardy

All plants are not created equal. Cool season vegetables are hardy souls that tolerate life in the temperate zone and grow from start to finish in the garden. On the other hand, warm season vegetables are native to tropical zones where the days are long and hot. They don't like extended bouts of cool weather and will stubbornly refuse to grow in anything but beachball temperatures. Warm season plants include tomatoes, peppers, eggplants, melons, cucumbers and squash.

Our job as northern gardeners is to trick warm season plants into thinking they're in Palm Springs. We do this by starting them indoors with heating cables and electric lights and then transplanting them to the garden once it's nice and warm.

As a rule, transplants should not go out in the garden until June first or later and even then, care must be taken to protect them from frosts and cold temperatures. The one exception to this rule is the cabbage family. Cabbage, broccoli, cauliflower and Brussel sprouts are transplanted to the garden in early April. They are hardy plants and don't need to be protected from frosts, but they are transplanted instead of seeded into the garden to hasten their maturity.

For small or medium-sized gardens (say less than 1500 square feet) it is easier to buy young transplants, called bedding plants, than it is to start them indoors yourself.

Buy bedding plants at nurseries or garden centers. Look for ones with good, healthy, green color and sturdy stems. Height is not an indication of plant vigor. Tall, skinny plants will actually grow slower and less vigorously than stronger, stocky plants.

Don't buy bedding plants too early. Cabbage family transplants, because they're hardy, can be planted outdoors as soon as they appear in stores, but others don't go out until much later. Get warm season plants just before you're ready to plant them.

It is important with all transplants, whether purchased or homegrown, to keep them growing. If put out too early in cold weather or if kept in small pots too long, transplants get weak and stop growing. Once this happens, it's a struggle for them to catch up to healthier plants. If you can't put bedding plants outside on time, transplant them to larger pots and water well to keep them growing.

Growing Your Own Plants Indoors

If you need plants for a large garden, you can grow them at home less expensively, in the long run, than you can buy them. Owning a hobby greenhouse makes the job easier, but it is possible to grow good quality plants in your house with artificial lights. You'll need to purchase a few necessary supplies but all of them, except the soil mixture, can be re-used every year.

SUPPLIES:

Seeds
Seed starting mixture
Seed flats, peat pots, plastic pots
Heating cables (if room is unheated)
Artificial lights
Benomyl fungicide

All of the above items are available at garden centers but you can devise some of your own materials to cut costs.

For the seed starting mixture, mix one part sand, one part peat moss or vermiculite, and one part sterilized soil. Sterilize the soil in a shallow baking pan in the oven at 140° for thirty minutes. Seed starting mixtures should be light and fluffy for easy seed germination and root penetration.

To make your own seed flats, cut half-gallon sized milk cartons in half the long way. You can also use aluminum foil baking pans or any other container that will hold an inch of soil. Poke drainage holes in the bottom of all containers.

If you're starting seeds in an unheated room, basement, or garage, use heating cables or mats to warm the soil. Both warming devices lie under the seed flats and plug into a regular electrical outlet.

Plants need more light than incandescent light bulbs (the ones that go in lamps) provide. Gro-lites are made for growing plants and they range in price from eight dollars up to thirty dollars. Regular shop lights are a cheaper alternative. Use two long fluorescent bulbs, one "warm white" and one "cool white," to provide the full spectrum of light that plants need. "Warm white" and "cool white" are printed right on the glass tubes.

Prepare the seed flats and, if necessary, place heating cables underneath the flats. In a large bucket or tub, moisten the soil mix thoroughly. Because it contains absorbent materials, the mix will take a lot of water.

Fill the containers almost to the top with the moistened planting mix. Drench the soil with benomyl fungicide (available as Benlate in stores) to prevent damping-off disease of seedlings. Use one-half tablespoon per gallon of water.

Make furrows in the soil about an inch or more apart, by pressing down firmly with the narrow edge of a ruler. Plant seeds in the furrows at the depth recommended on the seed packet, usually one-eighth to one-quarter inch deep, but closer to each other than is recommended because you will be transplanting the seedlings from the flat.

Very fine seeds are hard to keep track of. One method is to crease a piece of paper and pour some seeds into the crease. Pinching the folded paper together, tilt the paper toward the seed furrow and let the seeds roll one at a time out of the fold.

When all the seeds are planted, cover them with moist soil and press down gently.

Keep the soil moist but not wet. Use a mister or a sprinkling can with very fine holes in the nozzle. Heating cables cause the soil to dry out rapidly, so check the flats daily.

As soon as seedlings emerge, thin them to stand an inch apart.

51

Unplug the heating cables and turn the lights on and keep them on for twelve to fourteen hours a day. For a few dollars you can buy an electric timer that will turn the lights on and off at the same time each morning and night.

As the plants grow, it is imperative to adjust the height of the light fixture so that the lights are never more than six inches above the tops of the plants. If they're higher than that the plants will stretch toward the light, growing tall and thin rather than forming stocky, strong stems.

When the plants are about two inches tall, transplant them to larger pots. Use peat pots, plastic pots, clay pots or variations such as styrofoam coffee cups, paper cups, cottage cheese containers, bottoms of milk cartons, etc. Anything you use except peat pots, must have drainage holes in the bottom.

Fill these containers with moistened soil mix. Then water the seed flats well. It's easier to get plants out of moist soil than dry soil.

Using a kitchen fork, remove a block of two or three seedlings from the flats. Gently separate each plant, holding it by the leaves, and press it into its individual pot. Fill new, moist soil around it up to the first pair of leaves. Water well.

When all the seedlings are transplanted, clean the soil out of the empty flat and set the pots in the flat. Set the flats back under the lights, keeping the lights on the same schedule. Once a root system is established, it's okay to let the surface of the soil dry out between waterings.

If the plant leaves start to pale, feed them once a week with a very dilute solution of any houseplant fertilizer. Use about half the recommended rate for houseplants.

Plants grown in small pots get root bound after a while. They stay green and alive but they stop growing. Keep plants growing by transplanting them to larger pots when the roots grow out of the bottom of the pots they're in. Tomatoes, peppers and eggplants especially benefit from three or more transplantings before their final move to the garden.

Because tomatoes can grow roots from their stems, remove the lowest set of leaves and bury the stems up to the next set of leaves each time you transplant them. This makes a larger root system on the plant each time it's transplanted.

Curcurbit family plants—cucumbers, melons, squash and pumpkins—are the only plants that shouldn't be moved to larger pots once they're growing. Plant three seeds in a three-inch peat pot and, after they germinate, thin to one or two plants. Cucurbits grow quickly; start them just a few weeks before the last expected frost. After three weeks, begin to harden them off and then plant them in the garden. Plant the peat pot and all so as not to disturb the roots.

SPOKANE DATES FOR STARTING SEEDS AND TRANSPLANTING OUTDOORS

VEGETABLE	START INSIDE	TRANSPLANT TO GARDEN
Cabbage, broccoli, cauliflower, Brussel sprouts	MARCH 1	APRIL 15
Peppers	MARCH 1	JUNE 15
Tomatoes, eggplants	APRIL 1	JUNE 1-15
Cucumbers, melons squash, pumpkins	MAY 1	JUNE 1

Hardening Off

Early in life, indoor plants have it pretty easy with comfortable temperatures, good light and all the moisture and nutrients they need. Planting these tenderfoots right outdoors with no prior training can virtually kill them.

All transplants, whether purchased or homegrown, should be subjected to the hardening-off process. The process is a training program for plants to get them accustomed to the rigors that lie ahead, such as temperature extremes, bright sun, drying winds, and pelting rains. Most nursery-grown bedding plants are

53

hardened-off before they're sold, but always check to be sure.

At home, hardening-off begins with setting the plants outdoors for a few hours on a mild day. Put them in a place that's protected from direct sun and wind. The next day put them out for a while longer. Each day after that, put them out for a little while longer until, over the course of a week or more, the plants are adjusted to life in the wide open. Toward the end of the hardening-off process, leave the plants outside all night, but if temperatures drop below 40°, be sure to bring them back inside.

Planting Transplants

When plants are properly hardened-off and when the air temperature consistently reaches 70° during the day, it's time to transplant to the garden. (Of course, spring weather is never consistent about anything. Rely on season extenders when weather doesn't cooperate.)

Prepare the soil, measure the space required for the plants to mature, and mark the planting spots with stakes.

With a hand trowel, dig holes and mix a teaspoon of fertilizer into the soil at the bottom of the hole. Mix it in well so that plant roots do not sit on top of concentrated fertilizer granules. Add composted materials in and around the planting hole too. A well prepared planting site eases the transition from pot to garden for plants.

Minimize root damage by watering plants well before removing them from pots. Support the plant at the base of the stem and invert the pots to let the plant slip out. Some gentle tapping and tugging might be necessary.

Set the plant in the planting hole immediately and press soil firmly over the roots. Water well and add more soil as needed to fill in the hole. Then press down to form a slight depression extending a few inches beyond the plant stem to collect rain and sprinkler water.

Peat pots should be planted directly in the ground with the plant. Prepare the planting holes as for other transplants. Soak the pots before setting them in the ground. Backfill with soil and water

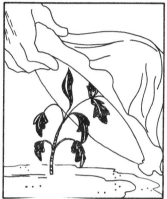

again. Remove any part of the peat pot that protrudes above the soil level so that it doesn't draw soil moisture away from the roots.

Set tomato plants deeper into the ground than they are growing in their pots. Remove the lowest set of leaves and bury the stem up to that point. Roots will grow from the buried stem tissue, enlarging the root system and enhancing the growth of the plant.

Put stakes for tomato plants in place at the bottom of the planting hole prior to putting the tomato in. This prevents root damage from jamming stakes through planted roots. Tomato cages are more expensive than stakes but cages support the plants and eliminate the need for fastening branches and shoots to the stake as they grow.

Water all new transplants well. Some gardeners swear by adding Vitamin B_1 solutions or Vita-Start to get transplants off to a good start, but others have had success without ever using the stuff. Adequate watering is probably the most important practice for successful transplanting.

EXTENDING THE SEASON
WITH PLANT PROTECTORS:
Getting the Most Out of Summer

We in the Inland Northwest are part of a large family of gardeners known generically as "northern gardeners." At our disposal we have special short-season vegetable varieties and an extra set of gardening equipment known as "season extenders" or plant protectors.

The purpose of plant protectors is to trick plants into thinking it's warmer than it really is. This is serious business and could mean the difference between red tomatoes and green tomato relish or ripe melons and meloncholy at harvest time.

Plant protectors can be as simple as a milk jug placed over an individual plant or as elaborate as a free-standing greenhouse. Between the two extremes are hot caps, tomato cages, row coverings, cold frames and hot beds, all of which can be constructed at home and re-used every year.

Protective coverings warm the soil and air immediately

around garden plants by several degrees, making it possible to put some vegetable crops outside two or more weeks ahead of the garden season.

All devices used to protect cold-sensitive plants get hot on clear, sunny days. Even when it is cool outside, the inside of plastic coverings can heat up enough to literally cook plants. Remember to remove or ventilate plant protectors when the sun shines.

Starting with the simplest and working up:

HOT CAPS, such as waxed paper tents sold at garden centers or plastic milk jugs with bottoms cut out and the lids removed, are coverings for individual plants. Hot caps protect new transplants from light frosts at night and from cold, windy daytime weather. They are helpful when plants are small and tender. Make modified hot caps that cover taller plants by draping a large, clear plastic bag over a wooden stake placed next to the plant. Hold hot caps in place with stones placed around the bottom edges.

TOMATO CAGES are sold in garden centers as cone-shaped wire frames to support tomato vines as they grow. Use these or design your own wire cylinders of heavy-duty screening with a four- to six-inch mesh. Cover the cage with a giant plastic bag or fasten thick plastic sheets around it. Tomato cages are larger and sturdier than hot caps and can accommodate larger plants. Design the cages with removable lids so that they can be ventilated on warm days. Later in the season when day temperatures are consistently above 70°, remove the plastic but leave the wire to support the tomato plants as they grow.

Variations of tomato cages are the unsightly but effective stack of black rubber tires and the retail product called "Wall-O-Water," both of which fit around the plant and warm the immediate vicinity.

Tomato cage   **Row covering or cloche**

ROW COVERINGS, sometimes called cloches, protect a whole row of plants or, if wide enough, a whole raised bed. Purchase long sheets of clear, four- to six-mil plastic at garden centers or building supply and hardware stores. Make hoops or arches over the garden rows with stiff wire or PVC pipe. Drape the plastic sheet over the hoops to form a long tunnel. Fasten one side of the tunnel down permanently but weigh the other side down with a removable stake so that the sheeting can be lifted back on clear days. Close off the ends of the tunnel with more plastic or wooden planks.

Use row coverings early in the spring and again in September and October to prolong the season for frost-tender vegetables.

A new DuPont product on the market is a spun polyester fabric called DuPont Lawn and Garden Blanket. Use it to cover wide rows or raised beds by fastening down the edges with soil or stones. Put it right over the soil without hoop supports. The Garden Blanket is light enough to be lifted by plants as they grow. It collects enough heat to warm the soil, protects plants from frosts, admits 80% of the sunlight (enough for plants), and prevents root maggots from infesting susceptible plants. Remove it after all danger of frost is past.

COLD FRAMES are like miniature greenhouses, designed for starting transplants, hardening-off transplants, or for growing early crops a month to six weeks ahead of schedule. Leave cold frames permanently in place near the garden or design them for temporary use each spring so that they can be folded up and stored when not in use.

Detailed plans for constructing cold frames are available at some county extension offices and in gardening magazines. Basically, take four planks of wood, about one or two inches thick, and nail them together to form a square or rectangular frame. Make the north side of the frame higher than the south side. Fit glass windows or heavy plastic sheeting over the top of the frame like a lid on a box. Because the north end is higher, the lid will slant to the south and collect more sun than a flat lid collects. Attach the lid to the frame with hinges so that it can open and close.

Plants seeds directly into the ground in a cold frame and transplant the young plants to the garden later or set pots and flats of plants in the cold frame for early growth and hardening off.

No heat source is used in a cold frame other than collected heat from sunlight. Close the lid of the cold frame at night, and, if sub-freezing temperatures are expected, cover the cold frame with a heavy blanket for warmth. Gallon-sized bottles of water set inside the frame will collect even more heat during the day and release it at night.

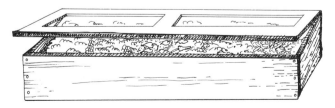

HOT BEDS are similar to cold frames except that they have an added source of heat such as heating cables lining the bottom or a 24-inch layer of fresh manure dug into a pit underneath the frame. Hot beds are used effectively in even the coldest gardening regions. If you're interested, look for a more detailed explanation in gardening encyclopedias or magazines.

MULCHING conserves soil moisture and keeps weeds down, but clear or black plastic "mulch" also raises the soil temperature considerably and thereby extends the gardening season.

Rolls of polyethylene film (a fancy word for plastic) are available at building supply stores and at some garden centers. Clear plastic collects more heat than black plastic, but it is not effective in preventing weed growth.

After preparing and fertilizing garden soil, lay the plastic along garden rows or over raised beds. Make X-shaped slits with a knife and set transplants in the center of the X. Make small holes in the plastic near each plant to allow water to get through.

Lengthening the garden season by protecting plants during cool weather is a must in many areas of the Inland Northwest. You can plant vegetables sooner for an extended harvest and you can grow varieties which, if they had their choice, wouldn't ordinarily grow here.

KEEPING IT ALL GROWING

You may consider it a natural wonder, but a vegetable garden is, in a sense, an artificial environment. Regularly maintained for optimum growing conditions, it's a far cry from a natural setting. Without your attention, however, few vegetables would make it to the harvest. Those that did would be skilled in survival tactics, not praise-winning productivity.

A gardener's summertime responsibilities include watering, weeding, mulching, feeding, and fighting bugs and diseases. The latter warrants a whole chapter by itself but the others are discussed here.

Watering

Once dry weather sets in, usually about mid-summer, watering the garden must be a regular practice. For loamy or heavier clay-type soil, especially if it's mulched, an inch and a half of water, applied weekly is adequate. Once a week, run the sprinkler until an inch and a half of water collects in the bottom of a coffee can placed in among the plants.

But gardeners with sandy or rocky soil low in organic matter will pale at the above suggestion. Watering once a week is sure death for their plants. Depending on *how* sandy the soil is, watering two and maybe three times a week may be in order.

Rather than going by the calender, go by the feel of your soil. Soil moisture below the surface of the ground is what's important. Once plants are established, don't be afraid to let the top inch or two of soil dry out between watering. Remember, plant roots need oxygen, too.

Watering is best done in the early morning. For one thing, there is less demand in cities or towns for water at this time of day, so water pressure is good. Also, cooler morning temperatures result in less water lost to evaporation. Watering at night is often associated with plant diseases because several hours of cool, moist conditions favor the development of disease organisms.

The point is to get water to the plants. Work schedules and

other demands on your time may not be conducive to watering the garden in the morning. Don't worry about it. Plants will take it when it comes.

Weeding

Weeds are tough, aggressive plants trying to "hold their own" against unwelcome visitors, i.e. your vegetables. They compete in the garden for nutrients and water and, if given an inch, they'll take a mile.

Regular cultivation, or hoeing, is imperative. There are no special skills involved except to avoid chopping off vegetable plants in the process. Keep the hoe sharp and the job will be easier.

As long as the weeds haven't flowered and made seeds, use them in the compost pile or add them to the mulch on the garden. If they've gone to seed, send them out with the trash.

Mulching

No discussion on watering and weeding a vegetable garden is complete without talking mulch.

Mulch is any material placed on top of the ground to conserve soil moisture and prevent weed growth. Once you use it, you'll never garden without it. It works.

Many different materials work as a mulch. A readily available source for urban gardens is grass clippings from lawns. Other natural sources include hay, straw, peat moss, sawdust, shredded leaves and wood shavings. Spread the materials between garden rows and in among plants.

The thickness of the mulch layer depends on the material used. An inch of sawdust will keep weeds down but three inches of grass clippings or five inches of straw are necessary for the same job. The lighter the material, the more you'll need.

Organic mulches are great because you can till them into the soil at the end of the gardening season to add organic matter and improve the soil structure. A few words of advice about using natural mulching materials, though:

1)   Wait two or three mowings after treating lawns with a weed killer before using the clippings as mulch. The herbicide may be transferred to the garden where it can kill or stunt vegetable plants.

2)   Don't put organic mulches on the ground too early in the spring. A mulch layer insulates the soil and keeps it from warming up. Seed germination and plant growth are delayed this way. Wait until the soil has warmed (usually May or June) before using mulch materials other than plastic.

3)   Use 1 cup/100 foot row of ammonium sulfate (21-0-0) prior to putting down sawdust or woodchips. Micro-organisms use a lot of nitrogen during the wood decay process and vegetable plants may temporarily turn yellow and stop growing when nitrogen is not available.

Using polyethylene film, or plastic, as a mulch is popular among some gardeners for its convenience and durability. Rolled out between rows early in the season or around the edges of the garden, the plastic warms the soil and prevents all weed growth. Weight down the edges with rocks or dirt and make slits in the plastic at regular intervals to let water through to the soil. Heavy-duty plastic can be rolled up and stored over the winter and re-used the following year.

Feeding

The adage, "If it ain't broke, don't fix it," applies to growing vegetables, too. If plants are green and growing vigorously, leave them alone. They're doing fine. In many gardens, where the soil is rich and fertile, fertilizing once prior to planting is enough to get plants through the season. Often, however, circumstances are such that plants don't thrive in the garden all season long. Bad weather, poor soil structure and fertility, overwatering and pest infestation all keep plants from doing their best.

Cool weather, not nutrient deficiency, may be the cause of poor growth. If the early summer weather is really lousy, plants stay small and yellowish regardless of how much fertilizer is added.

Fertilize poorly growing plants only after the weather is consistently warm.

Plants grown in poor soil (i.e. rocky, gravelly or clay soil with little organic matter) will doubtless show signs of nutrient deficiency. Stunted growth and yellow, purplish or pale green coloring are telltale signs. Help plants out before they lag too far behind. Use a complete fertilizer such as 10-20-20 or 10-10-10 according to directions on the package, but make plans to improve the soil with organic matter before the next garden season.

Any time plants aren't looking up to par, try to find out what the problem is (bugs, water stress, etc.) and correct it. Then feed plants to get them growing again.

Also fertilize in mid-season when you harvest one crop and plant another one in the same place. Nutrients may be in short supply in that area. Fertilize according to directions on the fertilizer package prior to planting the second crop.

When feeding grown plants, spread a tablespoon of fertilizer on the ground around each plant and gently scratch it into the top half-inch of soil. Then water well. Don't get any dry fertilizer on the leaves or it will cause burn spots.

Long rows of vegetables are more easily fertilized by side-banding. Make a narrow trench at least two inches to the side of each row and sprinkle fertilizer in the trench. Push dirt back over the trench and water the garden. Be careful not to cut into plant stems or uproot shallow-rooted plants.

Foliar fertilizers, such as Agro Fish 'N' Six, Alaska Fish Fertilizer or solutions of Rapid-Grow, Miracle-Gro or Triple-20, are a convenient way to fertilize growing plants. Just follow label directions for diluting the product in water and pour the dilution right around or over the plants.

Don't even THINK of using a fertilizer containing a weed-killer, such as Weed and Feed, in the garden. The "Weed" part of Weed and Feed will kill vegetable plants just like it kills weeds in lawns.

INTERCROPPING AND SUCCESSION PLANTING
Land Use Planning in the Garden

Getting the most out of your garden involves some land-use planning. Intercropping and succession planting are practices that use garden space more efficiently, extend vegetable harvest over a longer period of time, and discourage some pests.

Intercropping is the technique of growing small, fast-growing vegetables in among larger, slow-growing ones. For example, cabbages should be planted two feet apart from each other. But it may take 60 or more days for them to grow large enough to use all that space. Radishes, leaf lettuce, spinach and mustard are all smaller, fast growing plants that can be planted in among the cabbage plants. The fast-growing vegetables will be harvested before the cabbages get full-sized. Other slow-growing vegetables include, but aren't limited to, broccoli, tomatoes and melons.

Use seed packet information to help plan for proper spacing and timing. Don't over do it though. Overcrowding of plants results in stunted vegetables and poor yields.

Succession planting involves planting a crop after another one is harvested or planting small quantities of one crop in successive weeks to extend its harvest over a longer period of time.

Peas and leafy green vegetables are often gone from the garden in early June. Rather than leaving that space empty, use it for the later, warm season plants such as peppers, tomatoes, eggplants, corn and cucumbers. Then follow up with cold hardy crops during the fall. Here are three examples of good plans:

Plant Sugar Snap Peas (70 days) April 15th; harvest June 25th.
Plant Ace Peppers (60 days); harvest September 1st.
Plant Blue Scotch Kale (55 days) for winter soups; harvest October 15th.

Plant radishes (25 days) April 15th; harvest May 10th.
Plant Danvers Carrots (70 days); harvest July 30th.
Wait til August 30th and plant Northland Thickleaved Spinach (50 days); harvest September 30th.

Plant Fordhook Giant Chard (60 days) April 15th; harvest June 15th.
Plant Straight-8 Cucumbers (60 days); harvest August 15th.
Plant turnips (50 days); harvest October 2nd.

There are many other possibilities. Try them for a continuous, high-yield garden, using cool season crops at both ends of the season. Don't neglect to fertilize between crops.

You can also extend the harvest of some crops by planting small quantities every two weeks or so. Instead of having a long row of spinach all ready to eat at once, have smaller amounts ready every two or three weeks. Cool season crops such as radishes, lettuce and spinach can be planted this way while the weather remains cool. Stop during the hot months and resume later on for fall harvests.

Beans, corn and carrots can also be planted successively, but be sure to plan for the final plantings of beans and corn to mature before the first fall frost, as they are not frost tolerant.

One of the principles in organic pest control is to discourage the build-up of host-specific pests. Host-specific pests are the ones that only like one kind of food. Cabbage root maggots, for instance, only like cabbage family plants. Sections of the garden which are continuously planted in cabbage or broccoli, therefore, are a godsend to cabbage root maggots. If, however, other plants are interspersed among the cabbages, the root maggot problem is not intensified. Using quick maturing vegetables like lettuce and radishes helps diversify the garden. The same general principle holds true for all other plants and pests.

66

MAKING COMPOST
To Keep Your Sense of Humus

Think of a compost pile as a recycling center which turns raw organic matter—leaves, grass, kitchen scraps, weeds, sawdust, etc.—into "humus." Humus is soft, dark, moist earth, like the stuff you walk on in the woods or forest. It's decaying plant or animal materials. When you make humus in a compost pile, it's simply called compost.

When added to the garden, compost improves the soil by increasing water absorption, creating air spaces and providing nutrients to plants. Although you can buy peat moss and similar materials that do the same thing for soil, the raw materials for compost are free and readily available. If you have room somewhere, try composting.

Like any aspect of gardening, composting can be as simple or complex as you'd like to make it. The simplest way is to compost materials in a heap in one corner of the garden. Or, to hide the pile from view, make compost in a bin. Gardening magazines and larger books contain some elaborate designs for such bins.

Most gardeners choose a method somewhere between heaps and designer bins by using chicken wire and scrap lumber to enclose an area at least 4-by-4 feet. The composting process occurs in both sunny or shaded areas. Compost piles are built up of layers of plant materials, soil and fertilizer. Begin the pile with a bottom layer of coarse material like tough plant stems, corn cobs or shredded twigs. This coarse layer decomposes slowly and keeps the bottom of the pile aerated.

Next, add about eight inches of plant material, such as grass clippings, chopped leaves, green weeds, peat moss, coffee grounds or kitchen vegetable scraps.

Finally, add a two-inch layer of soil and if available, some manure. The soil layer contains micro-organisms that decompose the plant materials. These organisms however, need nitrogen to speed the process. If manure is unavailable, sprinkle a cup of nitrogen fertilizer over the soil. Ammonium sulfate, urea, blood meal and cottonseed meal are all examples of nitrogen fertilizers.

Build up the pile by alternating layers of plant material, soil and fertilizer. Add new materials as they become available. Keep the pile moist with occasional waterings but don't make it soggy.

Every week or two, use a pitchfork or spading fork to "turn" the pile. Turning the pile provides air and causes even decomposition of materials. The more it is turned, the faster materials decompose.

While turning the pile you'll notice that its interior becomes very warm. This is because active micro-organisms generate heat.

Shredded or chopped plant materials decompose faster than whole ones. Grass clippings don't need shredding, but leaves and coarser materials do. One way of chopping leaves is to run over them with a lawn mower. Garden shredders can be rented or purchased.

Compost is done when everything is uniformly dark, moist and crumbly. A 4-by-4 foot pile kept moist and regularly turned will be good humus material within three or four warm months.

Consider compost a rich and precious substance. (This may take some imagination when you look at it.) If you've got a lot, spread it over the entire garden, mixing it into the top few inches of soil. But, if your supply is limited, use it where it will do the most good to plants, such as in and around planting holes for transplants or along the seeding rows. Mix it with the top few inches of soil in the seeding rows.

Materials that should not be composted include:
— Weeds that have gone to seed. Seeds can survive and be transferred to the garden.
— Diseased or insect-infected garden refuse.
— Meat scraps. Meat, grease, and fat odors attract animals.
— Pet manures. Harmful parasites may be transferred to the garden.
— Grass clippings treated with weed killers. Wait two or three mowings before using grass clippings after using a weed killer on the lawn. Weed killers linger on to become plant killers in the garden.
— Pine needles. They take years to decompose and provide little nutritive value.

Composting does not have to be a difficult or time-consuming project. Start small and see how much you can make with just kitchen scraps and grass clippings. You'll be surprised at what nature can do about recycling.

FIGHTING BUGS AND DISEASES
ORGANICALLY AND OTHERWISE

It's a dog-eat-dog world out there and the garden is no exception. A variety of bugs and diseases vie for positions on your vegetable plants. Perhaps you've heard that the best thing to keep in the garden is your own shadow. While it is true that your presence and careful surveilance are the best defense against problems, there are certain situations for which you may want to enlist the help of pesticides—organic or otherwise.

First, consider the problems. There are three main things that go wrong with garden plants:
1)   Diseases infect them.
2)   Bugs eat them.
3)   Soil and weather conditions are so bad that plants won't grow.

Disease organisms in this part of the country include viruses, bacteria, and fungi. They get around by blowing in the wind, splashing in the rain, and hitching rides on tools, boot-heels and flying insects. They enter plants through wounds or pores and then make the plants sick. Sick plants wilt, turn brown, or keel over.

Bugs include anything that crawls and eats. Aphids, beetles, weevils, maggots, flies, moths and worms all fit the description. Some prefer roots and stems and others savor the leaves. Bug infested plants wilt, get eaten up, or keel over.

Of the thousands of species of fungi, bacteria and insects in the world, only a small number of each causes problems on plants. It's pretty hard to tell the good microbes (fungi and bacteria) from the bad ones but insects are easier to see. Try to determine which ones are actually causing problems. Pest control does not involve killing everything that moves in the garden.

More often than not, plant problems are simply a matter of poor growing conditions. They include compacted soil, too much shade, water-logged roots, low soil fertility, and improper use of fertilizer or weed killer. Rule out these problems before laying the blame on bugs or diseases.

70

Next, take a look at all the garden products on the shelf. Overwhelmed? Okay, listen up.

A *pesticide* is any product that kills or reduces garden pests. *Insecticides* get insects. *Fungicides* get fungus diseases. *Herbicides* get plants (weeds). They're all pesticides and they're either synthesized from chemicals or derived from natural sources.

Organic pesticides and biological pesticides, are usually considered one in the same. Organic insecticides, such as rotenone and pyrethrum, are made from poisonous compounds in plants. They are not necessarily less poisonous or less toxic than chemical pesticides, but they are made with natural ingredients.

Biological insecticides, such as Dipel or SEEK are solutions of living organisms which parasitize (kill) certain insect pests. Dipel is a brand name for a solution of bacteria, Bacillus thurengiensis (just remember Dipel), which parasitize and kill caterpiller or worm-type pests. It's a nice product because it doesn't harm other, possibly beneficial, insects and it's not toxic to humans or other animals. Bactur-L, B.T. and Thuricide are other brand names for Dipel.

SEEK is a solution of nematodes that parasitize soil insects such as root maggots, cutworms, wireworms, root weevils and grubs.

Other biologics are in the research and development stage of industry right now. Stay tuned.

Common synthetic garden insecticides include diazinon, malathion, methoxychlor, Sevin, Thiodan, and Chlorban.

Common fungicides for use in the garden include captan, zineb, benomyl, copper, sulfur, thiram, maneb, Bordeau mixture and others. The tomato and vegetable dust products contain one or more of these ingredients.

All pesticides, before they're released on the market, undergo an Environmental Protection Agency registration process. Years of research determine the toxicity, effectiveness and persistence of the product. Then the label is made which contains information about what the product kills, what plants it can be used on, how much should be used, when to use it, what precautions to take, plus a whole lot of other information not pertinent to the gardener.

Actually, every worthwhile bit of information is printed right on the label, but it is so small and technical that the most often asked question of nursery employees is . . . "does this stuff kill bugs?"

What you need to find out from the label is:
1) What does it control—bugs or diseases?
2) Which insects or diseases does it control?
3) Which plants can it be used on?
4) How much do you need to use?
5) When should you use it?
6) How long must you wait before harvesting food crops? (For instance, "broccoli (7)" means you must wait seven days after using the product before harvesting and eating broccoli.)

Nearly every insecticide label warns against using the product around plants in bloom or in the vicinity of bees. This is good advice. Bees are beneficial insects that pollinate our agricultural and garden food crops. Do all you can to protect them.

The pesticide label, though tedious to plow through, contains all the factual information you need. Follow it explicitly, never increasing the amount recommended and never using it on plants not listed.

Common Bug Pests in the Garden

Root maggots are small, ¼-inch long white worms that bore into the roots and lower stems of broccoli, cabbage, cauliflower and Brussel sprouts just below the soil surface. At first the young plants appear wilted. They stay small and droopy or they topple over. Few grow to maturity. Diazinon and Chlorban insecticide granules, worked into the planting hole at planting time may help control this pest. To protect young transplants from maggot infestation, use the lawn and garden blanket (see page 58), or cut a circle of stiff, water repellent paper about six inches in diameter. Cut into the center of the circle and make a hole slightly larger than the transplant stem. Then fit the paper circle around the plant stem so

72

that it lies flat on the ground. The paper disk prevents the female fly from laying eggs in the soil around the base of the plant early in the season.

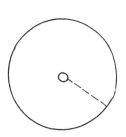 

Paper disk to prevent root maggot damage

Root maggots also affect radishes and turnips, but the paper disk method of protection is not effective on vegetables planted from seed.

Cabbage loopers and worms are long, greenish caterpillars, some with white or yellow racing stripes down their sides, that feed on the leaves of cabbage, broccoli, kale and other cabbage-family plants. They are easily seen and, if you're in the garden daily, you can handpick them off plants. Otherwise, insecticides Dipel, methoxychlor, malathion and Thiodan may help.

Paper tube or collar to prevent cutworm damage

Cutworms like all the vegetables. They feed at night and manage to stuff themselves with large chunks of leaves or even entire leaves. During the day these one- to two-inch fat, grey worms hide in the soil around the base of the plant. If you suspect their presence, gently cultivate around plants to expose them or use Dipel spray on the plants. One method of preventing cutworm damage to transplants is to wrap paper tubes or collars around the lower stem of transplants. A heavy, wax-coated paper like the kind used for milk cartons is best. Collars should extend from below the soil surface to an inch or more above. This keeps cutworms from curling around the plant stem and crawling up.

Tomato hornworms are giant, light green worms, gayly decorated with other pastel colors. They crawl around on tomato plants eating leaves and tomatoes. Handpick them off or use Dipel spray.

Corn earworms are unattractive green and black worms that feed on the developing kernels of corn. Eggs are laid on the new corn silks and the hatching larvae crawl up and into the corn cob. They feed to their hearts' content under the protection of the corn husks. Often their damage is confined to the top of the ear which can be cut off without interfering with further development of the corn. Mineral oil, applied with a medicine dropper inside the tip of each ear is said to suffocate the young worms. The insecticides Sevin and malathion are registered for use against corn earworms, but don't use it when pollen is shedding from the tassels of corn located at the top of the plant. Apply dusts only to the silks on the corn ears.

Wireworms are brown or yellow skinny, jointed worms with hard shells that live in the soil and feed on many different vegetables. They tunnel on and through root crops such as radishes, potatoes, beets, onions, turnips and carrots and they weaken young seedlings of beans, cabbage, corn and lettuce. Diazinon insecticide is registered but not always effective. Frequent cultivation will expose the worms to birds and other natural enemies. Wireworms may be particularly abundant in gardens that were recently converted from lawns.

Leafminers are hard to detect at first because you can't see them. They are tiny white maggots that tunnel between the upper and lower layers of leaf tissue. At first you may notice the mining pattern on the leaves but soon the damage looks like dead blotches on the leaves. Leafminers are problems in spinach, beets, chard and kale. Tear the blotchy leaves in half and you'll see they're hollow inside. Little white maggots wiggle around in there and their excrement, tiny black dots, will be present. There are no control measures other than removing infested plants from the garden. Also, get rid of lambsquarter weeds which are another host for this pest.

Spittlebugs get in just about everything from carrots to pine trees. You'll notice blobs of foamy wet stuff on plant stems or under leaves. Inside the "spittle" is a little yellowish bug that is hiding out from ultra-violet light. Spittlebugs cause very little damage to plants. At the nuisance stage, simply squirt them off plants with a garden hose. Control serious infestations with malathion, methoxychlor or rotenone insecticides.

Aphids will find their winged way to any and all plants. The small, ⅛-inch, green, yellow, gray, or red insects are usually seen in large numbers on the undersides of leaves or along stems of plants. They suck plant juices causing plants to turn yellow and sickly, sometimes with puckered leaves. Daily harsh sprays with water or insecticidal soap may keep the numbers down, but in problem cases, particularly on broccoli, Brussel sprouts and cabbage, insecticide sprays or dusts may be necessary. Diazinon, malathion, Thiodan and rotenone are all registered for use on aphids.

Mites are tiny 8-legged critters that feed during hot, dry months on the undersides of thick-leaved vegetables such as beans, cucumbers, squash, tomatoes and potatoes. The tops of leaves get mottled with bronze or silvery specks. Underneath the leaves, mites are busy at work making dusty, almost invisible, webs and sucking plant juices. Kelthane and diazinon are both registered for mite control.

Beetles of all kinds abound in a vegetable garden. The plant feeders eat holes in leaves. Asparagus beetles are black with yellow spots or red with black spots and they're about ½-inch long and slender. Cucumber beetles are similarly shaped, green colored with black stripes or spots. Colorado Potato Beetles are fat, ½-inch long and tan with thin black stripes down their backs. Flea beetles, which chew tiny holes in beans, cabbage, turnips, potatoes, tomatoes and peppers, are ⅛-inch round, black, jumpy bugs. Handpicking is possible with the larger beetles. All can be controlled with insecticides rotenone, malathion, Sevin, Thiodan or diazinon.

Weevils are similar to beetles but tend to be smaller and solid black, with long snouts. Pea leaf weevils eat notches out of pea and bean leaves. The larvae of pea weevils or pea moths may burrow into the pea pod and infest the individual peas. Malathion, methoxychlor and rotenone are all registered weevil controls.

Grasshoppers are prevalent some years and barely noticed in others. When they're profuse, it's hard to do much about them. Grasshoppers are migratory animals that eat and move on before others come in behind them. Malathion and Sevin are registered for control but not always effective.

Slugs are slimey brown or black creatures that slide across the ground and over plants like a big snail without a shell. They leave glistening trails along sidewalks or soil wherever they have been. This is a small tan variety, ½-inch long, that crawls in among leaf lettuce. Slugs, like goats and garbage disposals, eat anything. Various tactics are used to kill slugs. Among them:

1) Lay shingles between the garden rows at night. Slugs crawl under them to hide. Early in the morning, pick up the shingles and nab the slugs.

2) Squeeze Deadline, a toothpaste-like gel, on the ground in among the plants. Slugs succumb as they slide over it.

3) Put poisonous slug bait pellets of methaldehyde or mesurol under propped up boards or rocks. Brand names include Go-West Meal, Bug-Geta, and Snail and Slug Bait. (Use Deadline and bait pellets with caution as directed on the label.)

4) Bury half-empty beer cans in the ground. Slugs, attracted to the beer, fall in and drown. (This trick doesn't always fool slugs.)

Bugs That Help The Cause
(or at least won't hurt it)

Ladybug beetles are the saints of the garden bug world. They're cute, little, round, red beetles with black-spotted backs. The immature form is a purple and orange-banded larvae with black dots all over it. (No kidding.) Both larvae and adults eat aphids, so leave ladybugs alone when you see them.

Ground Beetles are those black beetles, about an inch long, that you see lying on their backs frantically kicking their legs as often as you see them in an upright position. They don't do much plant damage and they help out with decomposing organic matter. There's no need to kill them.

Centipedes and Milipedes with all the legs along side of them are organic matter feeders and harmless soil inhabitants. Leave 'em alone.

Spiders bear the brunt of many people's phobias. Actually, they catch and eat a lot of insect pests and they don't eat plants, so try to live with them in your garden.

Earthworms dwell below and aerate the soil, improving it for plant roots. In lawns, sometimes, they make hard mounds. For that problem, rent a roller to flatten them down for a few seasons, but welcome them to your garden.

Many garden magazines and catalogs advertize eggs of ladybugs or praying mantis or other insects known to be predators of insect pests. While these predators are indeed helpful in controlling pests, they hatch out with large appetites and wings. This means that if your garden isn't crawling with all the aphids they can eat, the predacious insects will simply fly to some other yard or garden in search of a meal. They feel no obligation to stay in *your* yard just because you bought them.

Common Diseases in the Garden

Powdery Mildew is a fungus disease which looks like a dusting of powdered sugar on leaves and stems of plants. The disease affects many different plants, shrubs and trees. Its growth is favored by cool, damp weather which occurs all spring, most nights, and much of the fall in most vegetable gardens. Plants are rarely killed by powdery mildew but sometimes leaves are stunted and deformed. Remove badly affected plants from the garden. On larger plants, such as squash, remove individual leaves that have mildew on them. A garden fungicide called benomyl or Benlate may be used to prevent powdery mildew but usually, by the time symptoms appear, it is best just to remove the plant.

Damping-off is a disease confined primarily to seeds and new seedlings. The disease organisms live in moist soil and rot the seeds before they germinate or infect plants as they emerge, causing the stems to rot and keel over at ground level. Use benomyl fungicide in seed rows or delay planting until the ground is a little drier.

Virus diseases also affect a large number of plants including most of the vegetables. Infected peas, beans, peppers, and cucumbers have small, distorted leaves, with a yellow and green mosaic or mottled pattern. Sometimes the leaves are puckered or crinkled along the edges. Tomatoes and potatoes get leaf-roll virus which stunts the plants somewhat and causes the leaves to get thick and leathery in texture. They roll downward along the vein. Viruses in corn stunt the plant and cause a yellow and green streaking pattern in the leaves. There is no cure for any virus-infected plant. Pull out and discard plants exhibiting viral symptoms. Look for seed or plant stock resistant to viral diseases. Commercial growers control insect populations of aphids, leafhoppers and whiteflies because these bugs can spread viruses from plant to plant as they feed.

Leafspots on tomatoes are caused by many different types of fungi. They start as small, brown circular spots which enlarge to form dead areas ringed by a lighter or darker shade of brown. Often they are harmless and do not call for any treatment. The older, lower leaves of tomatoes, for instance, always turn yellow and get spotted as the plant matures. Simply pull these lower leaves off. If, however, brown circular spots begin to spread upward on the plant and appear on newer leaves, suspect one of the tomato blight diseases. Avoid watering the tops of the plants, if possible, or use overhead sprinkling only in the early morning. Fungicide sprays or dusts can help check the disease. Other hosts for leafspot disease include peppers, potatoes and eggplant.

Bacterial leafspots on many different vegetable plant leaves differ from the fungus leafspots in that they are smaller, usually dark brown or black, and irregularly shaped. Bacterial spots appear first as watersoaked areas on the leaf. Later a yellow "halo" or ring surrounds the spot. Sprays or dusts are not effective on bacterial diseases. Remove infected or dead plants from the garden.

Potato Scab shows up on the potato skin as rough, scabby spots. Individual spots coalesce to form larger, corky areas. The disease is caused by a soil organism which is active in soils with pH 5.7 or higher. (Unfortunately, that's what many garden soils are.) Treating potato seed pieces with captan fungicide is minimumly effective. For better results, use resistant varieties such as Netted Gem, Norgold Russet and red Norland, or grow potatoes so that the tubers are not in direct contact with the soil. Dig a trench about 6 inches deep and 18 inches wide. Plant the seed pieces in the bottom of the trench no more than an inch below the soil. Then fill in the trench with clean straw or hay. The roots of the plant will grow in the soil getting water and nutrients, but the potato tubers will grow in the clean straw, away from the soil diseases. Water and fertilize as you would for normally planted potatoes.

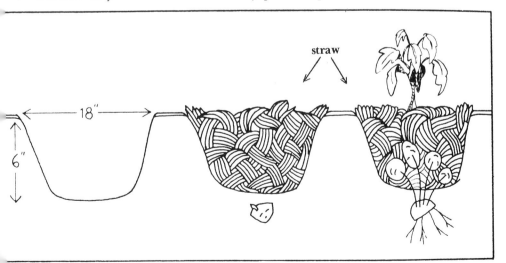

Problems Not Caused by Insects or Diseases

Cold Soil prevents vegetable seeds of most plants, especially the warm season crops, from germinating. Addition of fungicides and fertilizers can't help seeds that sit in cold, wet soil for a long time. Delay planting seeds until soil warmth is adequate. That's about 45° for cool season crops and about 60° for warm season ones.

Small, spindly plants may be the result of poor fertility, however, many gardeners are reluctant to thin young seedlings and overcrowding becomes a problem. Some leafy greens do not require thinning, but most others do. Follow advice printed on the seed packets for thinning young seedlings.

Bolting, or going-to-seed, occurs in cool season plants when hot weather arrives. Thick stalks shoot up which produce flowers or seeds. Nothing can be done once this happens. Stop planting that particular crop during warm months and replant it in late summer so that it can mature during cooler fall days. Use slow bolting or heat tolerant varieties such as Buttercrunch, Oak Leaf, and Salad Bowl Lettuce; New Zealand Spinach; Snow King Hybrid Cauliflower; and Savoy, Heavy Weighter Hybrid, and Harvester Queen Hybrid Cabbages.

Split cabbage heads and carrots occur when cabbages and carrots are left in the ground past maturity. The roots continue to supply water and nutrients to the plants which results in their splitting. Both carrots and cabbages can be left in the ground past maturity as long as their roots are severed and the weather is cool. Lift the carrots until root contact with the soil is broken and then shove the carrots back into the hole. For cabbages, use a spade to sever the thick root. Leave carrots and cabbages outside well into the fall and early winter months if indoor storage space is limited. After the first few hard frosts, cover the carrot area with a thick layer of mulch. This prevents the ground from freezing hard and makes it easier to dig up the carrots.

Knobby potatoes are a result of uneven soil moisture during growth of the tubers. Potatoes stop growing when the ground dries and then resume growth when water is available. The new growth

80

is often in separate knobs on the tuber. Maintain even soil moisture through the season by using mulch to conserve water and prevent fluctuating moisture levels.

Blossom End Rot on tomatoes is also caused by uneven soil moisture levels. Bottoms of tomatoes turn black or brown due to lack of calcium in the plant. Calcium is usually plentiful in the soil, but its uptake by the plant is impeded during water stress. Maintain even soil moisture as with potatoes. An immediate, but not permanent cure, is to spray the plants with calcium chloride.

Herbicides, or weed killers, kill all kinds of plants, not just weeds. Herbicides, with a few exceptions, do not belong in the garden. Never use Weed and Feed products in vegetable gardens. Some animal manures contain herbicide compounds. If animals are grazed on herbicide-treated pasture, the compounds can pass unaltered through the animal. When this manure is spread on gardens, the herbicide can damage vegetable plants. This is not common, but it does happen. Beware.

Herbicide-damaged plants are stunted and yellow and the leaves are cupped or puckered around the edges.

Fertilizer burn occurs when too much fertilizer or fresh manure is used. Leaf margins turn brown and dry. Leaves pucker and roll up. Plants stay yellow and dry-looking for quite a while. The best remedy is to water, water, water to leach the fertilizer out of the root zone. If you lose the battle, wait a while and replant.

Birds are usually good guys in the garden, feeding on insect pests. Sometimes, however, they take the notion to eat tender young pea shoots as they emerge in the spring. Netting or screen material placed over the row until the peas are five or six inches tall is the best solution. Noisemakers or scarecrows don't fool birds for long.

Underground rodents are indeed a nuisance when they move into the garden. Mechanical traps, available at nurseries and garden centers, are the only reliable recourse.

Without trying to paint the picture too black, there are many other things that go wrong in the garden. Ortho has a great, but expensive book called *The Problem Solver* with answers for every spot, bug or trouble you can imagine. *10,000 Garden Questions Answered*, published by Doubleday and Co., and *Organic Plant Protection*, by Rodale Press, also contain answers to frequently asked questions. Your local library doubtlessly has other helpful books.

Some counties in the Inland Northwest are fortunate to have Master Gardener Volunteers working during the spring and summer. These experienced gardeners, trained and sponsored by the state university, offer free advice on plant problems. Call your County Extension Office (see pages 24-26) to find out about the program in your area.

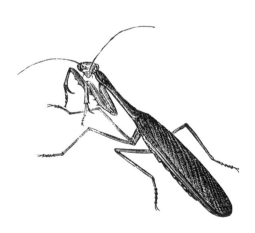

HARVESTING VEGETABLES

Harvesting must be done at just the right time to get vegetables at their peak of flavor and nutritional value, but the line between not-quite-ripe and overripe is thin indeed. Bulging beans, flowering broccoli, and bloated cucumbers are all signs of getting to the harvest too late.

A sure-fire way to pinpoint the day of ripening is to go on vacation. Vegetables will promptly ripen two days after you leave. If a vacation isn't in your plans, here are some pointers for picking vegetables just in the nick of time:

ASPARAGUS: Two years after planting (not any sooner!) harvest the spears that emerge in spring. Cut seven- to ten-inch spears with a sharp knife just below ground level. Harvest for about eight weeks. Don't cut any of the green ferny growth until it turns yellow in the fall.

BEANS (Green): Let the pods get full-sized but harvest before the beans inside begin to bulge.

BEANS (Dry): Let the beans inside the pod bulge and wait for the pod to dry. Then shell the beans (remove the pod) and allow them to dry out completely. Store them in a cool, dry place in glass jars or plastic bags.

BEETS: Two-inch diameter beets are good. Larger ones tend to be woody. Beet greens are ready when you are.

BROCCOLI: Cut off the main head while the little green buds are still tightly closed. Once the buds blow out into yellow flowers, it's too late. After the main head is cut off, side shoots continue to grow well into the fall. They're smaller than the main head, but no less delicious.

BRUSSEL SPROUTS: As each bud gets to be about an inch in diameter, cut it off the main stalk, removing the leaf underneath it at the same time. In late August, cut off the top of the plant to hasten development of the sprouts on the plant below. Cut to about fifteen inches in height.

CABBAGE: Cut when heads are large and firm. To prevent splitting of mature heads during the early fall, sever the main root with a spade or twist the cabbage so that root contact with the soil is broken. Cabbages may be kept in the garden longer into the fall this way. (Storing cabbages inside is difficult for one-refrigerator families.)

CANTALOUPES: Usually the vine starts to wither close to the melon as it reaches maturity and the melon separates easily from the stem. Check for ripeness by pushing in gently at the end of the melon not attached to the vine. Ripe melons are slightly soft here.

CORN: Pick ears when they feel well filled and the kernels are plump and milky. The silks should be dried and shriveled.

CUCUMBERS: Harvest when they're green, firm and of moderate size. Large, puffy ones are overripe.

EGGPLANTS: Pick when they're the size you want them. They are fully ripe when the fruit stem gets woody. Late in the season, pull off flowers and fruits which won't ripen to hasten development of ones closer to maturity.

GARLIC: Remove seed heads as they form in the summer. Bend the plant down when the leaves begin to yellow and dig the bulbs when the plant has dried completely. Store bulbs in a cool, dry place.

JERUSALEM ARTICHOKES: Dig tubers after first freeze when the plant is killed. Any tubers left in the ground will grow into new plants next year.

LEAFY GREENS: Pick leaves of lettuce, spinach, mustard, chard, etc. as soon as they look like salad material. Once they produce seed heads, they taste a little bitter, but are still edible.

OKRA: Pick when the pods are two to four inches long and snap off easily.

ONIONS: For fresh table use, pull up onions which are less than an inch in diameter. For storage onions, pull the bulbs as the tops yellow and die down. Dry them further in a warm, dry place. Store close to 40°:

PEPPERS: Pick when they're firm and shiny green, unless you want sweet, red ones. For red peppers, let them go as long as possible on the plant before the first frost.

POTATOES: Dig new potatoes when plants flower. Dig the larger tubers when the potato vines yellow and dry. Gently dig the tubers, being careful not to scrape or cut into the skin. Let them dry a little bit before brushing off the dirt and bringing them inside. Keep potatoes at 60° to 70° for a week and then store them in a cool, dark place, preferably with moist air, at 35° to 40°.

RHUBARB: Two years after planting, cut leaf stalks just above ground level when they're the thickness of a pencil or more. Harvest only for four weeks, then let the plant grow undisturbed. Remove and discard seed head when it appears. Rhubarb leaves are poisonous and should not be eaten.

RUTABAGAS, PARSNIPS, AND TURNIPS: Dig carefully after the first early frosts. For storage, cut off the leaves one inch above the crown. Keep them in humid air between 32° and 40°. Storage above 45° causes woodiness.

SUMMER SQUASH: Pick when the squash are moderately sized, well-colored and while the rind can still be easily dented with your fingernail.

WINTER SQUASH AND PUMPKINS: Leave them on the vine until after the first frost unless they're ripe well before that. They should have good, uniform color typical of the variety and the rind should not puncture easily. Cut them from the vine leaving two inches of stem attached to the squash. For long storage, cure in a warm place, close to 80° for about ten days, and then store at about 55°.

TOMATOES: Let the color get uniform and typical for the variety. (Some are yellow, some are pinkish, and some are deep red upon maturity. Refer to the seed packet.) Green tomatoes which have begun to change color slightly may be picked before a frost and brought indoors to ripen. There are many tricks to ripening tomatoes inside, such as putting them in a covered box, hanging the plant upside down by the roots, or wrapping each tomato individually in newspaper. Just setting them on a table or windowsill works too, and it's a lot less bother.

Vegetables, when they're ready, come on fast and furiously. Even the most attentive gardener will let a few vegetables get away, either from oversight or harvest burn-out. If this happens to you, pull the overripe ones off the plant anyway. It helps others to grow and ripen behind them.

85

PREPARING FOR WINTER

When it's all said and done and the plants have been picked dry . . . there's still more. The clean up.

Remove all plants and plant parts from the garden and throw them in the compost (discard real buggy ones). Then go back and cultivate the soil, getting rid of the weeds. Till in raw organic matter such as fresh manure, grass clippings, chopped leaves, straw, etc. Save already composted materials and fertilizers for the spring cultivation.

Now is a great time to take a soil test (see page 24) and add sulfur or lime, if needed, for pH adjustment.

You may choose to leave some of the garden intact. Root crops such as carrots, turnips, salsify, parsnips and Jerusalem artichokes can remain in their places well into the early winter months. Mulch over the tops of root crops to keep the ground from freezing hard. Also, cabbage, Brussel sprouts, broccoli, kale, savoy cabbage and Chinese cabbages are frost tolerant and will produce through the fall and early winter. Let these stay in the garden as long as they're willing.

If chives, rhubarb and perennial herbs are outgrowing their present location, divide them in the fall. Dig the whole plant up and divide it or force a shovel down through the top of the plant and divide the roots into two or more sections. Replant the sections and water them well until the ground freezes. Chives, rhubarb and asparagus do not need to be mulched for winter protection.

Leave a row or two open if you love garlic. In October, plant individual cloves about six inches deep and at least eight inches apart. Water well and cover with a few inches of leaves or grass clippings. (Make a note to remove the mulch layer in early spring.)

AND FINALLY, before you forget all your mistakes and lessons, make notes for next year's garden. Write down things like what vegetable varieties you liked, how much room plants took up, how much they produced, or anything else you'd like to remember. Tuck the notes in with next year's seeds, stored in a cool, dry place, so that you won't lose track of them. Without notes, you'll be surprised at how much you can forget over the long winter.

There is space at the end of this book for notes but you may prefer to keep a running account, year by year, in a small notebook.

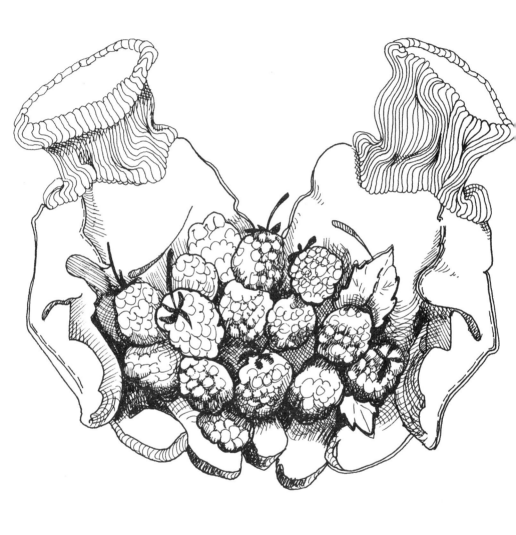

PART THREE

GROWING BERRIES, GRAPES, AND FRUIT TREES

BERRIES

Strawberries and raspberries are automatic inclusions in many gardens on the east side of the Cascade Mountains. Both are easy to grow and well suited to the climate and soil conditions here.

Blackberries and blueberries are desirable too, but not good choices for Inland Northwest gardeners.

Blackberries prefer a temperate climate with mild winters and a lot of moisture during the summer. The ideal situation for them exists over on the coast, which is where they are all growing. Profusely.

Blueberries need a very acid soil with a pH between 4.3 and 4.8. That condition doesn't exist naturally east of the Cascades and changing the pH that much is highly impractical. If you're determined to grow them, Earliblue, Jersey, Stanley, Blueray, Bluecrop, Ivanhoe and Colville are good varieties. Ask nursery employees for correct cross-pollinators and buy plenty of sulfur, aluminum sulfate or Miracid for soil acidification.

As for the strawberries and raspberries, both should be purchased as certified stock at local nurseries to ensure hardiness and health. The rest is up to you. This section contains information on which varieties to look for and how to grow them in a home garden.

Planting and Growing Strawberries

Strawberries come as Junebearers which produce one crop a year in late June, or as Everbearers which produce a June crop and an August crop. Total production from either type is about the same.

Strawberry varieties that do well in the Inland Northwest include:

Junebearers		Everbearers	
Earlidawn	Skuksan	Quinault	Streamliner
Premier	Totem	Ogallalla	Rockhill
Benton	Hood	Ozark Beauty	Tillikum
Olympus	Catskill	Brighton	Geneva
Northwest	Siletz	Hector	Red Rich
Rainier	Tioga	Fort Laramie	Gem

These are not exclusive lists. Other varieties may do well, but the above-mentioned ones come recommended from state universities and from the local nurseries that sell them.

Plant strawberries in the spring in well-drained soil where they'll get full sun. To avoid the Verticillium Wilt disease, don't plant them where potatoes, tomatoes or raspberries have been growing.

Work about ¾-pound of 21-0-0 per 100 square feet into the soil before planting. In areas where phosphorous and potassium are deficient, use a complete garden fertilizer, such as Morcrop or Tomato and Vegetable Food. Mix it well into the top six or eight inches of soil.

In raised beds formed with a rake and hoe, make furrows three feet apart. Set the new plants in the furrows two feet apart from each other. Spread the roots evenly around the furrow and cover with soil. Keep the crown, which is the thickened portion where roots and stem meet, right at the soil level. Do not bury it.

Water the row well and keep the plants watered regularly during the first two years. Use a mulch of grass clippings or black plastic between rows to conserve soil moisture and to smother out weeds.

Strawberry plants produce runners on long stems that sprawl over the top of the ground. A new little plant forms at the end of each runner and roots from it grow into the ground. Do not let any runners root during the first year. However, after that let the runners fill in the planting bed or row. When they grow out of the bed or between rows, cut them off. You need to be able to walk between the strawberry beds at harvest time.

Buds for the next year's crop are formed in late summer. For this reason always fertilize strawberries in late July or August, after the berries are harvested. Most eastern Washington soils, being adequately endowed with phosphorous and potassium, only require addition of 21-0-0. Apply about ¾ pound per 100 square feet every two years after harvest. Where soil tests indicate the need for phosphorous and potassium, use a complete garden fertilizer according to directions for berry plantings.

In very cold locations, where winter temperatures stay consistently below freezing, mulch over the strawberry plants in the late fall to prevent damage from the alternate freezing and thawing of the ground. Leaves mixed with straw or pine needles are good insulators. Leaves used alone tend to mat down and cause mold problems. Be sure to remove the mulch in the spring before new growth starts.

Diseases and Pests of Strawberries

DISEASES

There are several "unknown" diseases in strawberries. They may not be unknown to a plant pathologist equipped with a laboratory, but for all intents and purposes, a home gardener must be satisfied with names like wilt, blight, and decline. The life expectancy of the home strawberry planting is about five or six years. After that, plants start declining for one reason or another and yields are reduced. When this begins to happen, just throw in the towel and dig the whole bed up. Start over with new, certified plants. It is best to plant in a new area, but if your present site is the only possible one, remove all the roots and crowns and cultivate the area several times. Removing plants in the late summer and replanting in the spring is the best alternative to planting in a completely new area.

Following are some of the most common diseases affecting strawberries in the Inland Northwest:

ROOT ROTS are common if plants are watered too much or if drainage is poor. Leaves of plants turn yellow and wilt. Healthy roots are white and firm inside. Rotted ones are dark colored and mushy. Dig up and discard root rotted plants.

VERTICILLIUM WILT is a fungus disease which lives in the soil. The fungus invades roots and crowns, causing a reddish discoloration inside them. The whole plant stops growing and turns yellow. Older leaves curl up along the mid-vein. Remove infected plants and do not replant strawberries, raspberries, tomatoes, peppers or potatoes in the same place. These plants are all susceptible to Verticillium Wilt.

VIRUSES are microscopic organisms that get inside the plant and stunt its growth. Symptoms vary, but leaves are usually small and distorted and sometimes look crinkled around the edges. Sometimes they are streaked yellow and green. Pesticides are not effective on any virus disease. Pull up and discard infected plants. Avoid virus problems by using certified, virus-free plants and don't set new plants in among older ones.

INSECTS

ROOT WEEVILS are little white grubs that feed on the roots of plants early in the season. Use diazinon or SEEK in the soil prior to planting or scratch them gently around established plants if root weevils are found. Root weevil adults emerge as small, dark, hard-shelled insects. They feed on the leaf margins, creating a notched appearance around the edges. This leaf damage is harmless to the plants, but it does indicate the presence of the pest in the roots.

SLUGS: Same as in vegetable gardens. Several slug baits are marketed but Deadline is probably most effective.

SPITTLEBUGS: Same as in vegetable gardens. Their damage is generally undetectable. Wash them off with a garden hose.

LEAFROLLERS are green or brown worms that roll themselves up inside the leaves and eat the green tissue. Pick rolled leaves off and squash the worms inside. If infestation is severe, use insecticides Dipel or Sevin. Do not use Sevin while strawberries or surrounding plants are flowering.

MITES: Same as in vegetable gardens. Dusty appearance to undersides of leaves and bronzing effect on top are telltale signs of mites. Harsh soapy water sprays are effective, but difficult to do on undersides of leaves. Kelthane is a registered miticide spray.

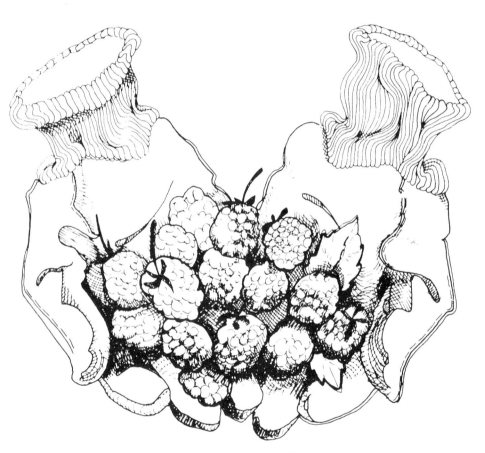

Planting and Growing Raspberries

Raspberries are easily grown anywhere in the east side of the Cascade Mountains. They require full sun, well-drained soil and a trellis or fence for support.

There are Junebearers, which produce one extended crop

every year, or Fall Bearers which produce two crops during the growing season.

Red raspberry varieties for Inland Northwest gardens are:

Junebearers			Fall Bearers
Meeker	Fairview	Sumner	Heritage
Haida	Puyallup	Chilcolten	Fallred
Newburgh	Skeena	Canby	September Red
Nootka		Willamette	Indian Summer

Munger and Logan are common black raspberries and Brandywine, Marion and Clyde are purple raspberries. They are planted and grown much the same as raspberries.

Start with certified raspberries and plant them in the spring. Incorporate manure, peat moss, compost or other organic matter in and around the planting holes.

Work about a pound of 21-0-0 fertilizer per 100 foot row into the soil. In areas were phosphorous and potassium are deficient, use a complete fertilizer according to label directions for berries.

Set the plants along a fence or wire trellis, spaced about three feet apart. If you're planting more than one row of plants, make rows about six or eight feet apart.

Keep plants watered well during the first season. Mulch with grass clippings or black plastic to keep weeds down. Weed competition can greatly reduce berry yields.

Raspberry plants are pretty tough plants. They don't require much special attention except for pruning which is necessary to keep plants from becoming a tangled mess. It's a very easy job when done annually.

In the fall, take a pair of hand clippers and go look at the canes. The ones that grew berries this year are brown and dry. Cut these off right down to the ground. They'll never produce berries again. The green canes grew up this year but produced no berries. Next year they'll have berries. Keep four or five of the thickest of these canes per plant and cut the others off at ground level. Also, remove any green canes that are trying to sneak out into the lawn or over to the other side of the fence. If the remaining canes are over five feet tall, cut them back or secure them to the fence or trellis so they don't lash around during winter storms.

In the spring, cut back all canes to stand about four or five feet high and remove any that got damaged during the winter.

Fertilize raspberries with ½ to 1 pound of 21-0-0 per 100 foot row in the spring as new growth starts. Fertilizing once every two or three years is all that's necessary in good soil.

Expect a home planting to last between five and ten years. They can grow longer than that but usually, because of virus diseases or just old age they start to decline in vigor, producing small and tasteless berries. When this happens, remove all the plants and start over with new, certified stock.

Diseases and Pests of Raspberries

DISEASES

VIRUSES are common and almost unavoidable after several years. Symptoms include small, misshapen leaves which are streaked or mottled with yellow and green and sometimes puckered. Berries get small and tasteless. Once the symptoms show up in one cane, consider the whole plant doomed and remove it. That's all you can do with virus diseases. No pesticides are effective on them.

CANEBLIGHTS are caused by several species of fungi. Canes discolor and crack, reducing the vigor of the leaves and berries. Prune out the infected canes and use a dormant lime sulfur spray on remaining canes in October and early March.

VERTICILLIUM WILT is the same fungus that infects strawberries. New canes wilt and the tissue just beneath the thin bark discolors. Remove infected plants and don't replant raspberries or related plants in the same area.

ROOT ROTS are similar to the ones infecting strawberries. Rotted roots are dark and soft and do not extend much beyond the stems. Leaves get small, yellowish and wilt easily. Avoid watering too often; once a week should be plenty. Look for varieties resistant to root rots when purchasing new stock.

INSECTS

ROOT WEEVILS are white grubs that feed on roots, causing plants to wilt. Use insecticides diazinon or SEEK in soil prior to planting or scratch them gently into the ground around established plants if root weevils are found.

CROWN BORERS are inch-long larvae that bore into canes at or below soil level. Canes swell near the base and eventually break off. Drench lower canes and soil with diazinon in October and early March. Treat for two years in a row to break the pest life-cycle.

LEAFROLLERS are the active little buggers that web and eat in leaves and sometimes fruit. Insecticides methoxychlor, Dipel and Sevin are registered for control. Do not use Sevin when berries or surrounding plants are in bloom.

GRAPES

Just as in buying real estate, the three most important factors in growing grapes are location, location and location. Grapes need a growing season, without frosts or freezing temperatures, of at least 150 days. While not all Inland Northwest regions have growing seasons that long, there may be specific locations called micro-climates, in every yard or garden where grape-growing conditions are met.

Search high and low for the best possible grape-growing site on your property. In short-season areas, the ideal site is on a south-facing slope, or against a south-facing wall or building. The goal is to catch the greatest amount of heat possible for these heat-loving vines.

Grapes tolerate a wide range of soil conditions. Sandy loam is the best kind, both for drainage and heat retention, but many grape varieties survive and produce in the sorriest of soils.

There are three types of grape vines. European grapes, called vinifera grapes, are the wine grapes. They require the least amount of water and soil fertility but they are also the least cold-hardy and the most susceptible to disease and insect pests.

American grapes are used mostly for juice, jellies and fresh consumption. They require better soil and more water than the vinifera grapes but they are hardier and more disease resistant.

Hybrid grapes are crosses between the European grapes for fruit quality and the American types for hardiness. They are suitable for wine making, jellies and fresh table use.

All grape plants are self-fruitful and do not require cross pollination. American and Hybrid varieties suited for the Inland Northwest are listed here. European varieties, the wine grapes, are also listed but they will grow successfully, with consistent grape production, only in areas with relatively long, warm summers and either moderate winter temperatures or where winter protection can be provided. White Reisling, Gewurtztraminer, Chardonnay and Pinot Noir are among the hardiest of wine grapes. Local wineries, if they grow their own grapes, can suggest the best varieties for your location.

European (vinifera)	American*	Hybrid*
White Reisling	Beta (B)	Himrod (W)
Chenin Blanc	Fredonia (B)	Foch (B)
Gewurtztraminer	Concord (B)	Aurora (W)
Grenache	Niagara (W)	Interlaken Seedless (W)
Chardonnay	Delaware (R)	Verledet (W)
Cabernet Sauvignon	Van Buren (B)	Cascade (B)
Semillon	Ontario (W)	Seibel varieties (varies)
Merlot	Campbell Early (B)	Gold Musat (W)
Sauvignon Blanc	Sheridan	Schuyler (b)
Pinot Noir	Portland (W)	
Black Monukka	Lucile (R)	
Thompson Seedless	Worden (B)	
	Seneca (W)	
	Caco (R)	
* B = Blue grape	W = White grape	R = Red grape

Buying, Planting and Growing Grapes

Purchase certified grape plants at a nursery in the early spring and trim off any long, straggly roots, leaving a root system about eight to ten inches long. Keep the roots moist until planting time.

Dig holes, six to eight feet apart, and deep enough to accommodate the root systems. Incorporate manure, peat moss, compost or other organic materials in and around the planting holes to provide some nitrogen throughout the growing season. Do not use fertilizer on grapes during the first year.

After planting, cut back grape vines to two or three buds coming off the main stem. The plants will look dismally small, but rest assured—it's for the best.

Keep the plants well watered and weeded during the first part of the summer. Later on, in mid-summer, cut down on watering and let weeds grow. The weeds will use up some of the soil moisture which helps the grapes harden off for the winter. Commercial growers sometimes sow a grain crop in between rows of grapes to take up some of the moisture and to till in later for organic matter.

Grapes fare better without much fertilizer. Liberal amounts of organic matter worked in among the vines will release small amounts of nitrogen over the growing season. If the plants look small and yellowish, and if the problem is not due to cold weather or too much shade, use ammonium sulfate, 21-0-0, at ¾ pound per hundred square feet.

Water grapes whenever the top few inches of soil dry out during the first couple of years. Mature vines should be watered during dry months but won't need regular attention. Stop watering in late summer to allow the vines to harden off for winter.

In the fall, after the leaves have dropped, water well one more time to prevent winter injury to the roots. This late watering will not cause the plants to resume growth.

Pruning Grapes

Pruning is the trickiest part of growing grapes. If large yields are not important to you, the job of pruning can be done rather haphazardly to restrain growth of the vines from overtaking fences, buildings, patio furniture or other scattered objects. To increase grape production, however, pruning should be done annually.

There are several methods of pruning grapes but for the home gardener's purposes, two general techniques are discussed here.

The first is for cold-hardy grape varieties planted in an area protected from winter winds. Provide a trellis to support the vines. A chain link fence or two parallel wires, one about two feet and the other about four feet off the ground, will do. During the first year, train one shoot to grow straight up to the first wire. This is the main

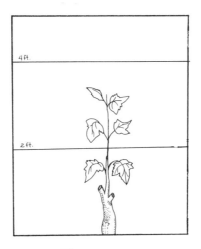

First year

trunk of the grape vine; tie it loosely to the wire or fence. Remove all the side branches in late fall.

The second year, let the main trunk grow up to the second wire or higher on the fence and let side branches grow. In the late fall, select four side branches, two on each side of the trunk, and train them laterally along the two wires or fasten them along the fence running parallel to the ground. At this point, the side branches are called arms. Prune each of the four arms back so that four or five buds are between the main trunk and the end of the arm.

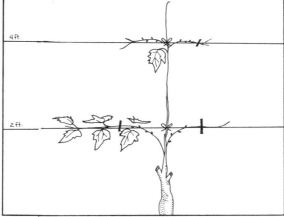

Second year

101

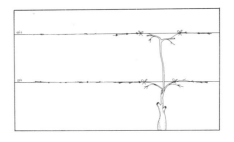

Third and every year thereafter

The third year, let the buds on the side arms grow out. In late fall, make four new arms by selecting two shoots coming off of each side arm but near the main trunk and cutting all others, including the original side arm off. Trim one of the shoots back to five buds. This is the new side arm. Trim the other shoot back to two buds. This, called the renewal spur, will be the side arm the following year. Use this pruning method of making a new side arm and renewal spur every year.

As the young plants begin to produce grapes, usually between the third and the fifth years, remove one half or more of the grapes. When the plant has produced a crop for a few consecutive years, stop removing grape bunches and prune side arms back to ten or twelve buds rather than five.

The second method of pruning allows for winter protection and is advisable for non-hardy varieties of grapes and where winter temperatures are severe. It is similar to the method already described except that the main trunk is cut off at a foot above the ground and all side arms develop below that point. At the end of each year, unfasten the side arms from the trellis and lay them down along the ground. Bury them in several inches of soil and use a mulch of leaves, straw or pine needles to insulate the soil. In the spring, when the soil thaws, uncover the vines and attach them again to their trellis. New side arms can be made from buds on the main trunk.

Regardless of how hardy a grape is or how protected it is, winters in the Inland Northwest are sometimes cold enough to kill most or all of the vine. Winter killed vines should be cut off at ground level. Sometimes the roots survive, especially if they've been insulated by a snow cover during the winter, and a new shoot will grow up. Grapes in the north are not grafted onto different rootstocks so go ahead and train the new shoot as you would a one-year-old plant.

102

Pests, Diseases and Problems

The number one problem you'll face as a grape grower is winter damage and periodic cool summers that won't mature a crop. After that, there are a few problems affecting grapes but they are hardly ever serious.

Gardeners in agricultural areas may find the widespread use of 2,4-D herbicide in field crops to be a problem. Homeowners who carelessly apply lawn weed killers near grapes are also to blame. Grapes are extremely sensitive to 2,4-D and other broadleaf weed killers. Herbicide damaged leaves appear frayed around the edges because the veins are distorted and "splayed." The whole leaf becomes misshapen and often cups downward.

Depending on how serious the damage is, it may or may not affect the crop. A few injured leaves are no cause for alarm. If many are damaged, about the only thing you can do is water the plant profusely and "wait and see."

INSECTS AND OTHER PESTS

LEAFHOPPERS: Light colored flying insects that hop more than they fly, suck plant sap from the undersides of leaves. Their feeding causes tiny white dots on the tops of the leaves. All the dots coalesce to form a dry, whitish appearance to the leaves. Serious infestations make the leaves dry and shrivel up. Control leafhoppers with malathion dust or spray, according to the product label.

SCALE INSECTS: Hard bumps along vines and shoots are signs of scale insects. Tiny insects emerge from under the hard shell covering in early summer and feed on plant tissue. Control with dormant oil spray in March or April.

MEALYBUGS: Ugly, blob-bugs, about ¼-inch long and covered with a white waxy or mealy coating, feed at the junctions of leaves and stems. If you catch them early enough, when they're really tiny, malathion spray may help control them. Otherwise, physically remove as many as possible, use dormant oil in late winter, and then spray early the following spring with malathon.

103

POWDERY MILDEW FUNGUS: This disease, just like on vegetables, coats the leaves and turns them white. If severe, it will distort the leaves and stunt their growth. Use sulfur spray to help prevent the disease. Also, water the vines at ground level so that leaves are not excessively wet.

BIRDS: Birds relish ripening grapes and will ignore any effort you make to scare them away. To protect grapes from bird raids, cover the entire vine with nylon netting or cover the individual grape clusters with paper bags held on with rubber bands. The grape berries don't need sunlight to mature so the bags won't interfere with ripening.

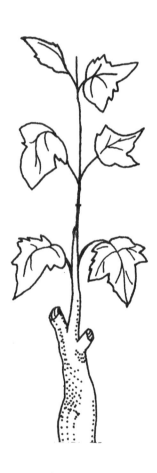

FRUIT TREES

Planting them is the easy part. Watching them blossom is the pretty part. Eating the fruit is the best part. But pruning and spraying are annual jobs that must be done for healthy trees and worm-free fruit.

Before choosing any fruit tree, ask yourself the following question: "Do I have the time and desire to take care of it every year?"

If you answered the above question, "Oh, yes! Yes, yes I do!" and you mean it, then here's what you need to know . . .

Choosing Fruit Trees

There are many different varieties of each kind of fruit tree. Because new varieties are always being developed and because the availability of varieties changes from year to year, it is impossible and impractical to list all fruit varieties here. However, you can still make the right decision when buying fruit trees if you understand a few basic things about all varieties.

Fruit size, color and taste are personal preferences, but other characteristics must be carefully considered for growing fruits in the Inland Northwest.

HARDINESS, the ability to withstand cold temperatures, is the key to survival for fruit trees. Choose varieties that can withstand the coldest winter temperatures in your area. Spokane's winter temperatures can dip to 30° below zero. Areas in northern Washington, Idaho and Montana get even colder. Of course, these temperatures don't happen frequently or even every year, but it only takes once to kill or damage susceptible trees.

Almost all apple and pear varieties are hardy to minus 30° or more, but the stone fruits — the ones with a pit or stone in the middle — are not. Some varieties of peaches, plums, cherries and apricots are hardier than others. Choose the hardier varieties and expect that in years with unusually cold winters or spring cold snaps, some fruit buds will be killed.

POLLINATION is what fruit trees claim as their sex life. There are male and female flower parts and pollination, the transfer of pollen to the ovary, must occur to make fruit.

Some trees are self-fruitful or self-pollinating. They don't need pollen from a different variety of tree to produce a crop. Wealthy and Golden Delicious apples, pie cherries, Stella and Starkcrimson sweet cherries, most peaches, most apricots and all European plums are examples of self-pollinating fruits. All other fruit trees need cross-pollination to produce fruit.

Mother Nature is known to throw a wrench in an otherwise smooth operation, and she's done it to make a few cherry trees cross-incompatible. Even though they're different varieties, Bing, Lambert and Royal Ann cherry trees will not pollinate each other. Plant a different variety with any of these trees. Also, don't depend on pie cherries to pollinate sweet cherries. While it may happen occasionally, the blossoming dates don't always overlap.

Another way to get pollination to occur for any fruit tree is to buy a tree with more than one variety grafted on to it, or tie a cluster of blooming branches from a pollinating variety into your tree when it's in bloom.

Most nurseries and county extension offices have charts describing pollinator varieties. Consult these to make sure you get two pollinating varieties when purchasing fruit trees.

TREE SIZE is an important factor in choosing the right fruit tree. Fruit trees come in standard, semi-dwarf and dwarf sizes, depending on the rootstock they're grafted onto. Standard trees grow to be thirty feet or more. This is too big for most backyard orchards and is highly impractical for pruning and spraying. Dwarf or semi-dwarf trees are easier to care for and they bear fruit at a younger age than standard trees.

Buying and Planting Fruit Trees

Buy fruit trees from a local and reputable nursery rather than through the mail. You can usually count on the variety being hardy for your area and you can inspect trees thoroughly before purchase. Also, you can buy when you're ready to plant.

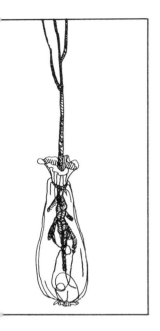  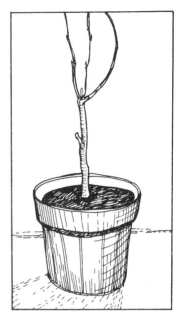

Trees are sold as bareroot, balled and burlapped (B&B), or containerized stock. For any kind of tree you buy, keep the roots moist and shaded from the time of purchase until planting.

Plant fruit trees in the spring as soon as you can dig a hole in the ground and preferably before the trees bud out. Plant them where they'll get full sun. Avoid planting them in a low area where cold air and frosts settle.

Dig a hole twice the size of the root ball or container and fill it with water. If the water doesn't drain away within a few hours, choose another spot. Fruit trees hate having wet feet.

Don't add much organic matter to the planting hole. Trees need to establish an extensive root system and if the soil right in the planting hole is too luxurious, the roots won't grow out into the native soil. It's best just to mix a little slow-release fertilizer, such as Osmocote or slow-release fertilizer tablets, into the soil you dug out of the hole.

After the site is tested for drainage, form a mound of soil at the bottom of the hole high enough for the new tree to sit on with its graft union above the ground level. The graft union is the crook at the lower end of the trunk where the tree is grafted onto the rootstock.

For B&B trees, remove any ropes or bands and pull the top of the burlap away from the root ball. It is not necessary to remove the burlap entirely.

Containerized trees come in plastic pots, metal cans or fiber pots. Plastic or metal containers, of course, should be removed. Fiber pots, although degradable, can present problems if they're planted in the ground. First of all, they take a lot of water to break apart and that amount of water may cause root rot problems. If, however, they're allowed to dry out they absorb moisture from the soil, depriving tree roots of water. To avoid potential problems, remove fiber pots too.

Set bareroot, B&B, or container grown tree roots on top of the mound in the planting hole. Fill in the planting hole with loose soil and tamp it down to get rid of air pockets. Water the area well and wait for the soil to settle in and around the planting hole; add more soil and water again.

Form a slight depression around the new tree to trap rain and hose water.

In windy locations, young trees, especially dwarf varieties, should be staked at planting time. Place a wooden stake next to the roots in the bottom of the planting hole before filling in the hole.

Use a soft tie of nylon material or rubber hosing to secure the tree trunk to the stake. Don't forget to loosen and eventually remove the tie as the tree grows, usually within three years.

Keep the trees watered regularly during the first two years. Once or twice a month, depending on your soil type, let the hose run slowly at the base of each tree until the ground is saturated. Deep watering encourages a deep, healthy root system.

Most newly purchased trees have several branches reaching straight up almost parallel to the trunk. Select three or four of these that are evenly spaced around the trunk. Cut the others off. Then spread the remaining branches with pieces of wood so that the branches make a 45° angle with the trunk. After a year or so, remove the wooden spreaders. Wider branch angles are stronger and allow for better fruit production.

Pruning Fruit Trees

Pruning makes trees grow more vigorously and produce more and better fruit. It increases the amount of light throughout the tree and keeps the tree at a manageable size for spraying and harvesting. Eventually, unpruned trees get dense with thin, unproductive branches that produce some pretty sorry-looking fruit.

There are entire books devoted to the subject of pruning in which different styles and types of pruning cuts are all graphically portrayed. Pictures do help but they never seem to look anything like the tree in your yard and ultimately the art of pruning is left to your own judgement. At first this is terrifying but with experience, you'll develop a style of pruning midway between timidly nipping at buds and recklessly sawing off branches.

A word of comfort here: it is almost impossible to over-prune a tree. Under-pruning is much more often the problem. So, be bold and with these guidelines, go out and prune your trees.

1)   Use sharp pruning shears and saws. Dull ones tend to gouge, gash and otherwise mutilate a tree.

2)   Prune in early spring before new growth starts. Pruning can be done at other times during the year without seriously damaging the tree but early spring is best because you can see the branch structure, remove winter-killed wood and stimulate new growth.

3)   Prune young trees lightly to shape the trees and direct growth outward and upward. Make diagonal cuts just above an outward reaching bud. (Read the last paragraph of the previous section for pruning brand-new fruit trees.)

slanted cut

4) Prune older trees heavily to remove weakened or dead branches and to stimulate new growth. Cut back on branches to keep fruit production closer to the tree and thin out some branches every year to increase light and air movement throughout the tree.

5) When removing large branches, cut close to the trunk or main branch. Don't leave branch stubs.

6) Don't paint pruning cuts. Trees do a remarkable job of healing themselves.

Young tree with too many branches

Same tree after pruning. Five side branches were selected to be main limbs.

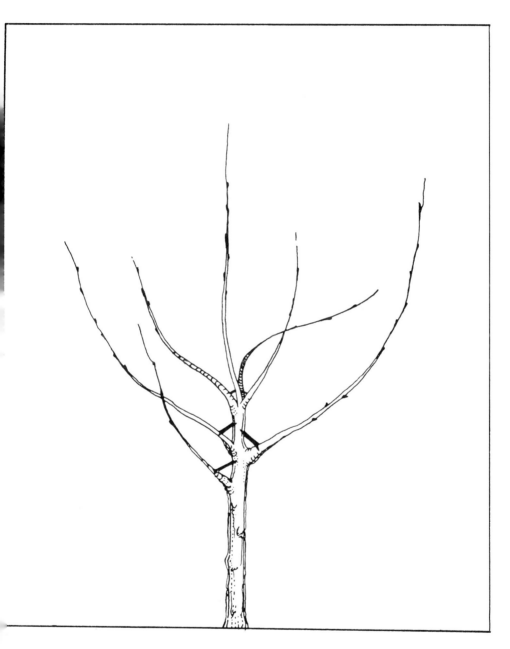

Young tree after wooden spreaders have widened crotch angles.

Pests and Diseases in Fruit Trees

You aren't the only one wanting to eat the fruits of your labor. Bugs and diseases do too. And you won't believe how greedy and ornery these pests can be until you try to grow fruit. You may be willing to put up with a few bumps and scratches on your fruit, but you probably don't want to sacrifice your whole crop to feed a bunch of worms.

Healthy, well-pruned trees are the first defense against invaders, but when push comes to shove, you'll need to enlist the help of insecticide and fungicide sprays. A few organic pest control tricks are helpful too. Refer to the information about pesticides in vegetable gardens. The concepts of pesticide action and safety are the same for all crops.

A good start at pest control on any fruit tree comes with using a dormant oil spray before the buds open. Dormant oil reduces trouble from scale insects, aphids, mites, and some diseases by coating and smothering over-wintering eggs and spores. Look for Volck Supreme Oil Spray, Dormant Oil, or Superior Type Oil Spray. Some dormant oils are mixed with insecticides for added control. Polysul Summer and Dormant Spray can be used, at different rates, during the dormant season and the growing season.

The following are the most common pests and diseases of fruit trees in the Inland Northwest:

LEAFROLLERS and *SKELETONIZERS* are greenish worms, ¼- to ½-inch long, with dark brown or black heads that roll up and/or eat the green leaf tissue. They attack trees in the early summer and infest ornamental as well as fruit trees.

APHIDS are small, soft insects, green, yellow or grey, that feed on new branch shoots or undersides of leaves. Leaves turn yellow and get puckered.

Aphids, skeletonizers and leafrollers, though discouraged somewhat by soapy water sprays, are best controlled with Diazinon insect sprays, spaced ten days apart. Mix diazinon with water according to directions on the label. If you're committed to soapy water, mix 1 tsp. liquid detergent or soap per gallon of water and spray daily or every other day while insects are present.

WORMY APPLES AND PEARS are the result of codling moth infestation. The female moth, about ¾-inch long and a mousy brown color, lays an egg in a young developing apple. The egg hatches into a cream-colored larva (the worm), which tunnels to the center of the fruit, turning it brown and mushy. The larva then leaves the apple, which may or may not fall off the tree. The escaped larva pupates somewhere on the branches and bark crevices.

In mid-summer, an adult moth emerges to begin the cycle over again. The second-generation larva leaves the apple and crawls into a bark crevice. There it will spend the winter.

Because larvae leave the apples before the fruit drops, collecting and destroying fallen fruit is not worthwhile.

Insecticide sprays help curb codling moth infestations. Diazinon, malathion, methoxychlor, rotenone, Zolone and Imidan are all registered for use on apple and pear trees. Generally, the recommendation is to spray the tree about ten days after all the blossoms have fallen off and to continue spraying every two weeks through July, but follow directions printed on the label of the product you have.

If you've got a lot of time and corrugated paper on your hands, there is a completely pesticide-free way of controlling codling moths. In mid-summer, wrap the trunk and main limbs of infested trees with a few layers of corrugated paper. The second generation larvae may crawl into the layers of paper to over winter. Then after all fruit is off the tree, remove the paper and burn or discard it.

Pheromone traps containing insect sex hormones are now available from some gardening magazines and garden product companies. These are sturdy pieces of cardboard containing a substance that attracts adult male codling moths. Males get caught in the trap and are unable to mate with females. The strategy here is to determine when the moths are out in strength and to limit spraying to those times, rather than spraying every two weeks for protection.

FIREBLIGHT disease causes the ends of apple and pear branches to die and droop over. Fireblight blackens leaves and bark until they look like they were scorched by fire. The blighted branches must be pruned off well below the darkened area. Sterilize the pruning tools with alcohol or bleach solution between cuts to prevent transfer of the bacteria responsible for the disease.

Streptomycin spray has been used in commercial orchards, but results have been unsatisfactory and cost for home use is very high.

APPLE SCAB is a fungus disease that causes rough, corky spots on the leaves and fruit of apples. A few spots may go unnoticed, but given the right weather conditions, spots can become numerous enough to deform leaves and fruit. Control Apple Scab disease with a fungicide spray such as Cyprex, Benlate, ferbam or ziram, beginning at the stage when a little pink color of the blossom shows between the bud scales, and again after bloom, according to label directions. The disease is most active during the spring rainy season.

POWDERY MILDEW is not often serious, but it usually manages to show up every year. It looks like a coating of powdered sugar on the new shoots and leaves of many fruit trees. It also infects flowers and vegetables. Affected leaves are small and deformed. Prune leaves off before the mildew gets too bad. A few fungicide sprays help prevent it, including Benlate and sulfur, but the effort is generally not worth it since the disease dries up and stops spreading in dry weather. Several varieties of fruit trees, roses, lawn grasses and even vegetables are now marketed that are resistant to powdery mildew.

WORMY CHERRIES are the result of visits from the cherry fruit fly. The life cycle of the cherry fruit fly is similar to that of the codling moth's. The adult female lays an egg in the cherry. The egg hatches into a maggot which eats into the center of the fruit. When the damaged cherry falls from the tree, the maggot burrows into the ground where it pupates over the winter. Adult flies emerge from the soil the following year between the end of May and early August.

Raking up and destroying cherries as soon as possible after they have fallen from the tree will cut down on the number of flies appearing the following year. But, if the cherries stay on the ground long enough for maggots to burrow out, raking up the cherries is ineffective.

Insecticide sprays for cherry fruit fly control include diazinon, malathion and rotenone used at ten-day intervals beginning in late May and continuing until two weeks before harvest.

Pheromone traps, similar to those for codling moths, are under study for pin-pointing peak flights of the pest. None are available at this printing for retail sale.

PEACH LEAF CURL fungus disease is the bane of peach tree owners because it is so prevalent. It shows up as red, thickened, puckered-up peach leaves, mostly on the tips of branches. The peach *fruit* is not affected by Peach Leaf Curl unless the disease goes uncontrolled for a few years. Then severe leaf damage results in a reduction of fruit yield.

It is frustrating that the time you see the disease is not the time you can do anything about it. The fungus spores over-winter on the bark and buds and infect new leaf tissue as it first emerges from the buds. To be effective, fungicides must be on the tree prior to bud break. Spray the trees in late February or early March. A post-harvest spray in October is also helpful in combating the problem.

Cyprex, Microcop and sulfur are effective sprays for Peach Leaf Curl. If you miss the pre-bud swell spray, there isn't anything you can do until the next year except pull off the worst leaf clumps and thin out the peaches to reduce demand on the remaining leaves.

The Redhaven variety of peach is more tolerant of the disease than other peach varieties.

CORYNEUM BLIGHT, BACTERIAL CANKER AND BROWN ROT are all common diseases of stone fruits, which cause ruptured bark tissue, called cankers, dark oozing sap and, eventually, dead branches. Pruning off the infected branches is an important method of controlling each disease. Timely fungicide sprays are helpful in fighting Coryneum Blight and Brown Rot. The three diseases are difficult to distinguish, but there are a few minor differences.

BACTERIAL CANKER affects cherry, peach and plum trees, usually before they're eight years old. The bark on branches, twigs or even the main trunk splits open and a dark, gummy sap oozes from the wound. Beyond the wound, branches wither and die. Prune branches back below the cankered area. If a canker is in the main trunk, the situation is rather hopeless. You can wait for the bitter end, which may take a few years, or you can start over with a healthy tree. The disease doesn't stay in the soil, so replant in the same place.

CORYNEUM BLIGHT is a fungus disease which shows up first as sunken, reddish, oval spots on the new twigs of peaches, apricots, cherries and plums. Peaches are most seriously affected. The disease also causes red or purple spots on the leaves. Often the spots dry up and fall out of the leaf which is why the disease is sometimes called "Shot Hole." Similar spots form on peach fruits. Cankers form on the older branches, causing swelling, rough bark and some oozing of dark-colored sap. Buds are killed and branches, infected with the cankers, eventually die.

To control Coryneum Blight, prune off infected branches and spray the tree in October and before bloom in the spring with sulfur spray, Captan, Bordeaux or Microcop. (Do not use sulfur on apricots.) Follow label directions for spraying.

BROWN ROT BLOSSOM BLIGHT is another fungus disease affecting cherries, peaches, apricots and prunes. Blossoms affected by this disease turn brown and wilt, as if they were frozen. Later, mature fruits get covered with a grey mold, shrivel up, and either drop from the tree or hang on as "fruit mummies." Twigs of Brown Rot-infested trees develop cankers similar to those with Coryneum Blight.

To control Brown Rot Blossom Blight, prune off infected twigs and mummied fruits to reduce the amount of infection spores on the tree. While the tree is in bloom, spray with Benlate, Captan, sulfur or other fungicides labeled for Brown Rot control. Spray again later, as the fruit ripens. Follow label directions for spraying. (Do not use sulfur on apricots.)

Clear or amber colored globs of sap on stone fruit trees are no cause for alarm. It is when oozing sap is dark-colored and associated with swollen branch wounds that a disease might be suspected.

WINTER KILL, causing dry dead branches and/or buds, occurs when winter temperatures are severe enough to freeze non-hardy wood tissue or when late spring frosts and cold snaps damage developing buds and branch tips. Check for damaged buds by cutting them in half with a sharp knife. Inner bud tissue will be blackened if the buds are damaged. Check for winter kill on branches by scraping away some of the surface bark on the affected branch. If the underlying tissue is brown and dry, chances are it's been cold damaged. Prune those branches just below the discolored part. Winter kill hardly ever does in an entire tree if it's healthy to begin with and, unlike diseases, winter damage doesn't get worse as the season progresses. Cold damaged trees usually go on to produce a good crop of fruit unless more than 80% of the fruit buds are killed.

Harvesting Fruit

Nothing tastes better than tree-ripened fruit. Pick it on a sunny day and let the juice dribble down your chin and you'll swear life has nothing better to offer.

Knowing when fruit is ripe can be as simple as tasting it, but there are a few definite signals if you need a more calculated answer for preserving or marketing reasons.

Red and yellow apples have what's known as a background color. Green apple varieties have it too, but it's difficult to see. The background color is the portion of the skin that doesn't turn red or yellow as the apple ripens. The area around the stem and streaks in the apple are such places. As apples ripen, the background color changes from bright green to a lighter green or yellow color.

Inside a ripening apple, the color of the apple meat changes from a greenish white to a yellowish or softer white. Also, the seeds in ripe apples turn brown when apples are ready to harvest.

Apricots, peaches and plums are best ripened right on the tree. When ripe, they are brightly colored and feel soft when *gently* squeezed. If peaches, apricots or plums are picked before fully ripe, they will ripen and soften at room temperature but they won't taste as sweet as tree-ripened fruit.

117

Cherries, on the other hand, must ripen on the tree. They won't change much after they're picked, so taste a few to be sure they're ready.

Pears are the sticklers when it comes to knowing when to harvest them. (Remember Mother Nature's wrench?) Pears don't ripen on the tree and if they're left hanging there too long, they get kind of gritty tasting and mushy around the core.

The best clue for knowing when to pick pears is that the fruit, with a gentle twist, pulls easily off the branch. Pears will still be hard at this point, but bring them indoors to room temperature and they'll be soft, juicy and delicious in about a week. If you want to store pears for a longer time, put them directly in the refrigerator after picking. Take them out about a week before you want them to ripen and they'll be just like the fresh picked ones.

All types of fruit ripen first on the south side of the tree. Keep this in mind if you don't want to harvest everything at once. Also, each variety of fruit ripens on its own schedule. If you have more than one variety of apple, cherry, peach, etc., check individual trees for ripeness.

INDEX

119

NOTES

NOTES

NOTES

NOTES

COLOPHON

The Tonie Jean Fitzgerald GARDENING IN THE INLAND NORTHWEST was printed in the workshop of Glen Adams in the sleepy country village of Fairfield, which is located on the north edge of the Palouse farming district, southern Spokane County, Washington state and one township removed from the Idaho line. The text was set in twelve point Baskerville type by Dale La Tendresse using a model 7300 Editwriter computer photosetter. The indexing was by Tonie Fitzgerald. The photography-darkroom work was done by Tami K. Van Wyk using a model 660C DS computer driven camera. The film was stripped by Dale La Tendresse who also made the printing plates. The sheets were printed by Robert La Tendresse using a 28-inch Heidelberg press, model KORS. Folding was by Garry Adams using a 22x28 three-stage Baum folding machine. The books were assembled by Sharyn Brown and Tami K. Van Wyk. Paper stock is seventy pound Island Offset, a Canadian sheet. Binding was by the News Review plant in Moscow, Idaho. This was a fun project. We had no special difficulty with the work.